You
whi

PIGEON RACING

PIGEON RACING

WILSON STEPHENS

WARD LOCK LIMITED·LONDON

Acknowledgments
The author and publisher would like to thank Dorian
Cross for drawing the line diagrams and for his
invaluable assistance with the photographs; Mr and
Mrs Jim Curry for allowing their pigeons and loft to be
photographed; and Peter Longhran for taking the
photographs for the book.

169093

First published in Great Britain in 1983
by Ward Lock Limited, 82 Gower Street,
London WC1E 6EQ, a Pentos Company.

Layout by Bob Swan
House editor Helen Douglas-Cooper

Text set in 11/12 point Melior

Set, printed and bound in England
by Netherwood Dalton and Co. Ltd.

British Library Cataloguing in Publication Data

Stephens, Wilson
  1. Homing pigeons
  I. Title
  636.5'96   SF469

ISBN 0-7063-6197-0

Contents

1 Home-based and nationwide

Nowhere can we see a pigeon race. Yet every Saturday from April to September pigeon races are flown to most towns in Britain and to many separate districts in all major cities. Pigeons are trained for racing at an estimated quarter of a million lofts, spread nationwide. Since about half of these have birds racing in any one week, and it is normal for each owner to make four or five entries, about half a million pigeons are in action every race day. On a peak summer Saturday the total will be higher.

Betting, in the familiar manner of bookmakers and odds, is not done. The sport has its special system of pools for competitors only. Through them a winning owner may make £2,000 on a race, in addition to prize money. This sum is comparable to the rewards of run-of-the-mill horse racing, though such a coup is rare because few pigeon owners make the necessary investment, most being in the sport for its excitements and pleasure rather than for profit. Even so, when trophies in kind such as motor cars for the winners of major events are considered, the rewards in pigeon racing are approximate to those in show jumping. How does it happen that so substantial and far-flung a sport can go on, for more than a century, virtually unknown except to those concerned in it despite the size and complexity of the organization behind it? And what is it that through changing times, in which economic conditions and life-styles have become so suddenly different, commands so much lasting enthusiasm from so many people?

The reasons for the enthusiasm are threefold. First, the zest for competition which is in most of us; secondly, the deep-felt need for the companionship of living creatures, which is sharpened by the deprivation from natural contacts with them caused by industrialization and the urbanization of modern life; thirdly, what can only be described as the magic of racing pigeons themselves, their beauty, their courage, their intelligence, and their inclination towards Man. The reason that the sport goes unnoticed is that pigeon racing is home-based. Despite its 250,000 active followers, it is a sport without public locations. By its nature, it could not use them. So it lacks a spectator element, having only participants; yet it has a public image.

Only a few years ago there was visible evidence of pigeon racing at any railway station. From baskets stacked on trolleys awaiting loading would come a melodious cooing which made many an uncommitted traveller peer in at the intriguing inner community of glowing eyes and lustrous plumage. Those hallmarks of the avian athlete make racing pigeons, as we shall see, very different from any other pigeons, wild or tame. But they are not now seen on their way to a race or training. The railways no longer carry them.

By the decision not to do so, a major change was signalized in the pattern of pigeon racing. Throughout its century's history, its character as a working class sport had been jealously guarded. Not that all its devotees are or ever were working class. Far from it. For reasons which will emerge doctors, clergymen, farmers and very rich businessmen have traditionally been part of the pigeon racing community. Even kings have taken part; Queen Elizabeth II still does. But its homespun psyche has remained firmly rooted in the manual ranks. There has been no keeping up with the Joneses; the pigeon folk have kept back with the Joneses instead, refusing to leave any of their number behind. The effect, perhaps the purpose, has been the maintenance of a communal spirit in which nobody need feel out of place. Those entering it from other backgrounds have always been welcomed, thanks to the recognition by all that material affluence brings no advantages. Into this outlook the railways fitted neatly.

For most of that century railwaymen were the aristocrats of industry. Moreover, railways had almost invented pigeon racing; certainly they had made it possible. Until trains provided the reliable, quick, cheap transport needed to move large numbers of pigeons to distant places, widely organized racing could not happen. The railways opened up all Europe to the Belgian, Dutch, French and German pioneers of the sport and, soon afterwards, the English, Welsh, Scots and Irish realized that all Britain was likewise opened up. Wherever a man wished to send his birds had suddenly become accessible.

Railwaymen, living close to their work and seeing the pigeon traffic day by day, naturally joined in. To be a railwayman and not to have pigeons was almost an eccentricity in some areas. Moreover, railwaymen had access to railway buildings. In pre-nationalization days the private companies, valuing the business gained, lent accommodation to pigeon racers for their pre-race formalities. Railways and racing pigeons became an unofficial partnership. When it was dissolved the sport lost much else beside its link with the consciousness of the wider public.

Everybody knows that the pigeons are taken to a distant point, released, and then fly home. But where is 'home'? All their homes are different. Each flies back to its own. So there can be no communal winning post. In addition, some of the homes to which the birds return must be nearer the start than others. Therefore a conventional race, bird against bird, is impossible. The race has to be against time.

If the birds were racing to lofts in a small and concentrated area of, say, a three-mile radius, the simple times of arrival could give a result within the limitations of rough justice. And so they did in the earliest days. A three-mile radius was, indeed still is, approximately the residence zone of the members of a club centred on a country town or a suburb. So at club level, and at the start there was no other, the first bird home was automatically the winner. This, to those taking a first view of the sport, might seem right and natural.

But the first bird home might, because of the location of its loft, have flown a shorter distance than the next; and the winning margin might have been only a matter of seconds. Such situations arose repeatedly. It became necessary to find some more sophisticated measurement of performance, especially in races open to more widely separated competitors than the members of a local club. So velocity replaced time as the criterion which decides a race. This enables the distance factor to be absorbed in the calculation.

The effect is that pigeon racing has been able to outgrow its small beginnings as contests among groups of local friends until now its organization is nationwide, and its events half-nationwide. The 'half' arises from facts of geography. The routes along which races are flown are known as 'roads' (railway vernacular inherited from the sport's formative years). British races are flown 'north road' or 'south road' or 'east-west'. Competitors who live in, roughly, the southern half of the United Kingdom tend to send their birds to the Pennines, Scotland, Orkney and Shetland for release — i.e., they 'fly north road'; those living in the northern half send their birds to Southern England, France or Spain, and thereby 'fly south road'. Those living in the far west race from the Low Countries, across the breadth of England, hence 'east-west'. Some fly both north and south roads, and a few all three.

These expressions, and others, are important to understanding conversation about the sport. Like all subjects dear to their enthusiasts' hearts, pigeon racing has its own language. Pigeon racers refer to themselves as 'flying men' rather than 'fanciers' to maintain their distinction from pigeon shows, and reflecting the days when 'flying' was a masculine preserve. Now some of the 'flying men' are feminine. In any case wives, sweethearts and sisters already had a long and honourable tradition as partners and backers-up in the running of racing lofts. Similarly, the place from which the birds are released is known as as a 'race point'.

Only in very exceptional circumstances are race points ever varied; not merely the town, but the precise position in the town at which release takes place. This is a consequence of the exactitude and scope of pigeon racing's modern background organization. Before pigeons can take part in a race the position of their home loft is plotted to within ten yards on the largest scale Ordnance Survey map. This plotting is then integrated into calculations of each individual loft's distance from each official race point. The calculations are sophisticated, being based on the Great Circle system which governs aerial navigation, long range artillery fire and nuclear weaponry.

The race points, from which each loft has its distance fixed, have their own place in the sport's traditions, as do race courses like Aintree, Epsom and Ascot on the turf. The mere mention of race points starts flying men talking — Northallerton, Perth, Thurso and Lerwick for the north-roaders; Templecombe, Weymouth, Nantes, Bergerac, Pau and Barcelona for south-roaders; Antwerp and beyond for east-west. The result of a race from any of them, expressed in terms of velocity, is likely to make pigeon racing realities even less comprehensible to those who do not know its technicalities.

The velocity formula is yards per minute. On hearing that a bird won a race from, say, Barcelona by half a yard, the listener may well conclude that this margin after 700 miles or so indicated something near a neck-and-neck finish. What is meant is that the winning bird's average speed was half a yard faster in every minute of flying time than that of the bird placed second. This, over the distance from Barcelona, is decisive superiority.

Since the results of all races, great and small, and the destinations of the pools money, depend on such mathematics, the organization which administers them is crucial. To have a high degree of accuracy in distance calculation would be meaningless if the time recording was not equally accurate. And no amount of care in either of these directions would earn respect if the possibility of "a fiddle" remained. To say that dishonesty is impossible in pigeon racing would be unrealistic; dishonesty is never impossible, even where it has not previously happened. It has in fact happened in pigeon racing, and men have gone to gaol for it. But the rules and the precautions, not to mention the traditions of sportsmanship and honest dealing, are strong enough to make it exceedingly difficult and correspondingly rare.

Pigeon racers are self-governing. Though many of them give much time and effort to committee work and organization, and though others become part of the sport as administrators not competitors, the sport has neither dictatorship nor an élitest level. Its structure is based on 'the clubs', meaning the local clubs to one or more of which every pigeon racer must belong. Clubs have a social side as well as a sporting function. In a pastime that has a high level of total involvement, they generate a warm, neighbourly and family spirit in which, significantly, pigeon racing in modern conditions becomes more and more a family sport.

Above club level are the Regions, the intermediate tier which unites all clubs in a given area; and parallel with them are Federations and Combines, co-operatives which exist to help clubs in the organization of races. Above the Regions are the national unions (see page 65). These unions have the three functions of policy making, rule enforcement and administration. The latter is the solid base for all the safeguards which keep pigeon racing straight.

Where money is involved, and where the performers are not people but creatures who can neither speak for themselves nor be cross-examined, safeguards are paramount. They begin with the unalterable identification of each individual racing pigeon by the fitting of official, non-removable, metal numbered leg-rings. Every owner orders an allocation of rings annually through his club, the figures on these rings being registered against his name. Each bears the initials of the registration authority, the number of the bird wearing it, and the year of its birth. The ring is put on the young bird's leg within ten days of its leaving the egg. At that age, the bones and muscles of the foot are not fully formed, and the toes can be passed through the ring. A few days later they cannot be, growth having eliminated flexibility. Hence the ring cannot be removed without destroying it (and losing the identity of the pigeon), nor can it be substituted. When a racing pigeon passes from one ownership to another, the number is re-registered accordingly. Thus is identity established beyond dispute, the first safeguard against mistake or fraud.

Before a pigeon flies in a race a second numbered ring is put on. This, being made of rubber, can be stretched to pass round the now fully developed foot and can be removed in the same way. The fitting of the race ring is one of the crucial events of 'marking night', the essential formality before the birds leave for a race point. The others are the testing, setting and sealing of the clocks, and the 'pooling' of each bird, designated by its number.

Theoretically, each flying man has his own clock. In practice, clocks are often shared in partnerships or by friendly arrangement between neighbours. The clocks are specially designed so that, once set, started and sealed, there can be no interference with their working. The clock has no

A pigeon-racer's clock face. The insertion of the thimble containing the race ring marks the time on the revolving time scales.

dial, but an aperture into which 'thimbles' can be inserted, the time of the insertion of each thimble being recorded internally. As each pigeon reaches its home loft its rubber race ring is removed, put into a thimble, and the thimble inserted into the clock, which cannot be opened without breaking the seal. Only race officials are entitled to do this. These are the further safeguards of validity in the timing system. From the arrival timings recorded in the clock, the velocities of each bird are calculated and the placings and pool dividends worked out.

Collectively, flying men therefore compete for their own money, and collectively finance their own sport. The more successful recoup through the pools something more than their investment, the unsuccessful something less. When the rate of loss exceeds the value of the pleasure gained, some people give up the sport. However, the compelling interest keeps many in the contest who have no illusions about their prospects of more than occasional success. At the top it is the habitual winners who take each other on. Big money cannot make a man a better flyer, or protect him against being excelled by those who, though less well off, are more thorough or more gifted in the management and training of their birds. Herein, perhaps, lies the mainspring of the sport's appeal, and the central question of what is needed for success. Men win if they, as well as their pigeons, are good enough, not unless; and there is nothing in pigeon racing to keep a good man down.

The basic requirement is plain stock sense, the gift of making creatures happy and healthy, these two conditions being dependent on each other. Though the details obviously vary, the knack is the same for the trainer of racing pigeons as for the trainer of racehorses (a significant number of famous people being masters of both arts, including Sir Gordon Richards, Jack Jarvis and several leading jockeys). Trainers of gundogs, sheepdogs, greyhounds and police dogs, and stock farmers of any kind, all need the insight which gains the confidence of the creatures they deal with, and gives them a sense of security. They need, too, the practised eye for spotting a need before it has actually arisen so that relaxation and contentment, the greatest of all the necessities for high performance livestock, are never interrupted. Pigeon racers need all this and something more.

Among flying men it is common knowledge that some of them not only possess these talents to a greater extent than others, but that for no perceptible reason pigeons will consistently fly better for one man than for his rivals. His are the first to press on with determination when a race settles down after release, the last to take it easy in the final long homeward miles on a hard day, hence the most likely to be a few invaluable seconds ahead when the clocks are opened, the sums done, and the lists made out. How this human power of attraction is acquired and expressed cannot be defined; it is invisible in itself but all can see the effect.

Although pigeon racing, like all sport, is competitive, it is also much bound up with stability. This helps to explain why, in an era superficially far from ideal for a stay-at-home pastime, it continues to grow. Its expansion more or less keeps pace with the growth of the population, not fast but steady. The social trends of the last three decades would be expected to produce a shrinkage, but the opposite has happened.

Recent generations of pigeon racers inherited the traditions of the Industrial Revolution, when country dwellers displaced by land enclosures moved in millions towards new opportunities in towns. Despite the relative prosperity they at first found there, they felt strongly their isolation from the natural scene and their loss of contact with living creatures, so kept pets as reminders of their old life. Often, for reasons to come, pigeons were chosen and pigeons were eventually raced by flying men who, until recent years, lived under much the same restrictions as did their forbears in Victorian times.

Then, men lived where they worked; and where they worked, they stayed throughout the year. Annual holidays were for the priveleged only; a week lasted six days of labour, and the Sabbath. Pigeon-racing, the sport of total commitment and home-based, fitted the need as nothing else did. Now times have changed. Mobility and leisure have become universal. Those who in the old days became pigeon racers almost inevitably to fill a gap in a dull life, now have counter-attractions such as weekend trips to the coast, caravan tours, Sunday outings for stock-car racing, sailing and golf, annual holidays often abroad, all undreamed of by earlier followers of the sport, and all incompatible with the need to wait by the loft to time in a bird 'pooled through' for a nice pick-up on the strength of his tireless wings. Yet the evidence is that despite the counter-attractions there are as many flying men as ever.

Perhaps more. There are many signs that the best of both worlds is being had on the basis of teamwork. Racing pigeons are not for fathers only nowadays. The whole family helps with the feeding and care of the birds, with the training and the paperwork. The commitment is no less, but it is more widely shared. The mobility and the leisure are there in some measure for all, given the necessary mutual support. For the same reasons, partnerships increase; so do arrangements whereby pigeon owners who are in fact rivals share the same loft. To some people it may sound like hard work. It is. But flying men would reply that such people do not know what they are missing.

One of the remarkable facts about pigeon racing is its non-regionalization. A popular myth is that it is primarily a north country sport. The figures show that the greatest concentration of pigeon racers is in Greater London, because that is where the greatest concentration of the population is. There are likewise great concentrations of flying men in the industrial Midlands, in the Pennine towns, in the Geordie country of the north-east, and the steel and rugby valleys of South Wales. Flying men are more scattered, but pro rata, through farming England, crofting Scotland, even in the far-off Hebrides, and among the green hills of Ireland.

2 High-mettled racers

Between men and birds there is generally a wide separation. Birds are warm-blooded reptiles, humans are mammals. We therefore have much more in common with animals, sharing, for example similar processes of reproduction and of rearing our young. We, and they, are products of a later stage in evolution, and therefore theoretically higher life forms. Birds originate much further back in time. The species now familiar to us had become established ten million years ago, whereas the time when our ancestors stood up and walked, thus becoming distinct from four-footed animals, can be traced back less than three million years. Birds became birds before the human race had a place on our planet, and have developed without inheriting a consciousness of our kind.

Hence humanity and birds co-exist, but do not team up in the manner by which master-and-servant relationships have been formed between man and dogs, horses, camels elephants, cattle, sheep, goats and cats. Any individual of these animals can be humanized with little difficulty: responsive to a particular human voice, appreciative of the human presence, and amenable to human will for reasons other than the expectation of being fed. But after an equally long history of domestication, man is no nearer to individual co-operation with hens, ducks and geese than he was to start with. Pet birds are kept in cages not only for their own protection but because, if they are not, they will fly away, regardless of the devotion lavished upon them.

There are a few exceptions to this generalization, and the most notable is the pigeon, and in particular the racing pigeon, the most highly developed pigeon of all. Unlike other birds, it is possible to form a man-pigeon relationship by mutual consent, similar to the man-dog relationship, in which the pigeon's regard is not only that for mankind, but for one individual man. It is also one in which the man in question can discern evidence of another intelligence interlinking with his own, creating and reflecting a regard for each other which deepens with time into trust and interdependence. It is from this firm joint interest, rather than from the bleak concept of a mere homing instinct, that the sport of pigeon racing devolves. A homing instinct undoubtedly does exist, and pigeon racers have found that by selective breeding and careful education it can be developed into something more, a homing technique, which the best racing birds must consciously use. This will be discussed at greater length later.

Considering the discoveries which archaeology has made about the ascent of man, the closeness of this link and the use that can be made of it are not surprising. Nobody knows whether the pigeon or the dog was man's first friend as he rose above the other creatures of the primeval world. All three were cave-dwellers. Dogs attached themselves to the family circles of the cave-men, earning their keep as sentinels and scavengers, while the blue rock pigeons, ancestors of all our domestic breeds, returned at night to the ledges overhead, roosting there as they still return to the cliff caves on the coasts of Scotland and the Hebrides.

To share caves with Stone Age man would not seem particularly attractive to wild birds free to go elsewhere. But it has been proved that this is what they did, despite the disturbance and the smoke rising from the camp fire below. The scene is in keeping with the voluntary habits of feral pigeons today. No species of wild pigeon is shy of man. They do not move out of their accustomed home areas when men move in, as was often demonstrated in World War II by the green pigeons of Burma, which kept to their roosts when armies clashed in what had until then been uninhabited mountains. Pigeons whose once domesticated ancestors reverted to the wild do not seek the open countryside. They remain in man's company, even in the densest urbanization. Every city in the world, from the Poles to the Tropics, from Moscow to Los Angeles, has its resident population of 'streeters' and, no matter where, the type is always the same. In human affairs the pigeon is ubiquitous; where men settle, there he is. Even ring doves, with the woods and fields of the home counties open to them, infiltrate fifteen miles of suburbia and inner London to make their homes in the squares of Mayfair and the City, nesting on the window ledges of the Houses of Parliament.

In doing so, they are responding to the attraction which has kept us and them together across the ages. For them, we appear to generate a fellow feeling; for us, they fulfill a longstanding satisfaction. They (as fancy breeds, not racers) were an enthusiasm of merchants along the Silk Road from China into India in the time of Marco Polo; the first fantails in Britain were a gift from Akbar the Great of India to Queen Elizabeth in the sixteenth

Head of a racer: (a) the bill, short and strong; (b) the wattle and (c) the cere, both snowy white; (d) a generous skull, not mean or pinched, on which the feathers have a plum-like bloom; (e) the eye, of any colour between deep ruby and pearl, its expression bold but calm.

century; short-faced tumblers which could not feed their own young were being bred in Smyrna at the time of the Crusades, proving 800 years of man-managed foster-rearing. There is nothing new about the bond between men and pigeons. The racing pigeon is the culmination and the perfection of it.

The subtlety of the difference between them and other pigeons must be the dominant impression on an observant person seeing racers for the first time. Perhaps, to some people, there is no difference, except that racing pigeons look cleaner than the rest. They are much the same size, have similarly coloured and patterned plumage as all pigeons. But to those with an eye for livestock, and the insight for looking rather closer, the differences are great.

Physically, the most obvious of them is the back. Racing pigeons have the strong, flat ramrod backs of athletes, or of those whose work demands hard muscular condition. This impression is heightened by the fusion of several central vertebrae, so that the middle section of the spine is rigid. That other telltale, the clean set of shoulders is there, too. So is the crisp, alert movement when walking. Look now at the head — that head which we believe (we cannot prove) contains one of the most fascinating of all

Nature's secrets, the means by which pigeons find their way home. Though there is no scientific confirmation of the hypothesis that a large head contains more or better brains than a small one, it is a fact that the heads of well-bred racing pigeons are more generously proportioned, more domelike above the eyes than the meaner skulls of chance-bred 'streeters'. More probably this stems from their more prosperous ancestry and careful rearing, the undoubted superiority of the racer in surmounting the problems and hardships of direction, weather and distance having no visible indication. There are, however, well recognized marks of quality and well-being associated with the head.

The wattle, the cuticle surmounting the upper bill at its base, is well-developed and snowy white in a hard-trained racing bird. So is the cere, the similar cuticle surrounding the eye. The feathers of the head, short, close-lying and disregarded by some because they play no part in flight, are a valuable guide to well-being. They should lie flat, smoothly upon each other. When they do not, and begin to 'stare', a sure signal of ill-health or discontent is being given. It is on the head feathers that the 'bloom' is seen, that powdery appearance which is born by ripe sloe berries. Continuing downwards, it merges with the irridescence of the neck feathers to become the high gloss which tells of regular exercise, good living, and the right ancestors. Most arresting of all the features of the head is the eye.

A racing pigeon's eye is a subject for connoisseurs. The eyes of any creatures, ourselves included, do not merely allow the possessor to see out; they let others see in. From the eye, perhaps even through the eye, we can weigh up the character of another man, a horse or a dog; through the eye we can see the inner pigeon. It is, indeed, as singularly beautiful an eye as exists in the whole range of Nature, lustrous with a jewel-like glow, richly coloured in shades of red varying from orange through brown to almost black. A full, bold, generous eye reveals a pigeon possessing those courageous, intelligent and steadfast qualities without which the most perfect physique is useless amid the stresses of a race. Later, we shall see what these stresses are. Many flying men believe that close study of the eye can reveal the 'eye sign', which indicates the pigeon's capability in route-finding. This point also will be discussed in more detail later. For the present, consider the physique, and how it can be perfected.

Again take first impressions. Prominent among them must be wonder that anything so small can be capable of the tremendous feats of flying which are achieved week in, week out; not merely by race winners, but by tens of thousands of their rivals, repeatedly, every season. The same could of course apply to migrant wild birds but migration flights, remarkable as they may be, are not performed at a speed of 500 miles or more per day,

Left *A racer's wing topside, showing the length and breadth in proportion to the bird's body-size, and the strength of the flight feathers. Reading from the top of the wing's rear edge, note the ten primaries, then the secondaries, and under the thumb the bastard wing.*

Right *The wing, underside, extended to show the elevation from which the propulsive down-stroke starts.*

regardless of weather. Moreover, they take place only twice a year, and the long interval between them gives ample recovery time. Racing pigeons not only cover long distances very fast, but with so little strain on their constitutions that after a week or two of light exercise most of them are fit to do it again.

The components of a racing pigeon have been refined by evolution and selective breeding to achieve the highest possible quality in the basic requirements, with nothing superfluous. These components are wings,

Pigeon colours: Above This is a blue, sometimes known as a blue-bar from the feather pattern of the wings. The same colour distribution occurs in reds, though sometimes the red equivalent of the blue-bar is known as a mealy.

Above right This is a blue chequer. The same pattern of patches of the basic colour on a lighter background also occurs in reds, the other primary pigeon colour.

Right This is a grizzle, a colour variety often regarded as likely to be tough, hard-flying racers. Other popular racing patterns are pied (white patches, especially on the head), and gay pied (more white than colour). Less popular as racers are black, velvet, dun, and tricolour. These colours occur spasmodically, hence are regarded as possible evidence of chance breeding.

feathers, bones, muscles, heart and lungs, digestion, brain and will power. All pigeons are bold and dashing flyers and their lightweight skeletons are exceptionally strong by avian standards, having been developed during the evolutionary millenia to withstand exceptional stresses. In the wings the length ratios of the various bones, which otherwise correspond to those of the human arm and hand, are such that the fully extended wing is disproportionately long for the bird's body size in comparison with other pigeons. Since the wing is the basic instrument of success or failure in a race, consider it more closely.

Not only is it longer, but it is used with greater force and in longer strokes than the wings of almost any other bird. The joints permit a 180° arc of

movement for each wing, their extremities touching both above and below the bird in wing-beats of maximum power, as when speed is being built up after take-off. Their exertion of force against the air is so great that feathers of less than the highest quality would disintegrate under the strain. The ten primary flight feathers in each wing are the direct agents of propulsion, corresponding in effect to the oars of a racing crew or hooves of a racehorse, and maintenance of feather quality is a crucial part of racing pigeon management. All feathers are changed each year and success in the next season's racing is impossible unless the new feathers are satisfactorily grown. The dates of the shedding and the emergence of the primaries can be predicted with great accuracy, and govern the occasions on which a bird is fit to race.

While the ten primary flight feathers in each wing exert the pigeon's driving power against the air, the secondaries have a balancing and stream-lining role, while a single-feather appendage to the leading edge, control-led by a separate muscle linkage and known as the 'bastard wing' is thought to have an air-braking effect when the bird is landing. Each wing beat, which to the unaided eye looks simple, has been revealed by slow-motion photography to be a complex series of movements involving millions of interacting parts. As wing action and feather function are the means by which racing pigeons produce their decisive attribute, speed, they deserve examination in depth, though necessarily briefly.

All the forward impetus of the airborne racer is produced by the down-strokes of the wing, the up-stroke being merely the recovery in preparation for the next drive forward. The great power of the down-stroke originates in a mass of muscle anchoring on the breastbone, so strongly developed that in a hard-trained racing bird this muscle alone constitutes one third of its body weight. The effect is to drive the primary flight feathers, which have a springy quality similar to whalebone, hard against the air, levering the bird forward and through it. In order to conserve energy for these forward thrusts the up-stroke must expend as little energy as possible, which means eliminating air resistance.

For this reason, the up-stroke is not made with the wing extended and rigid, as in the downstroke. The lift of the wing begins at the elbow which, by rising first, presents a peaked entry into the aerial slipstream around the moving bird. The secondary feathers then act as a fairing, deflecting eddies round the bird's body as the primaries are raised butt-first, spilling the air away over their points which, until a late stage in the stroke, remain inclined downwards.

This energy-saving process is reinforced by the feather structure. A microscope reveals that the fibres which, by branching outwards from each quill, compose its web are themselves barbed. When exerted against air pressure below, the barbs interlock. Each feather then presents a solid surface, like an oar. But when the air pressure below is eased, as when the wing begins to lift into an up-stroke, the interlock is released and the web of the feather becomes permeable by air from above. As the feathers overlie each other to form separate propelling instruments and areas of cladding, it will be seen that their character can alter according to need, being at one moment air-resistant and at the next air-admissive. A single primary feather carries about 1,000 fibres, each of which has many barbs, so the number of reciprocating moving parts in operation at every wing beat add up to millions for each pigeon.

The organs of the pigeon's body which give it driving power depend for their efficiency on qualities inherited from each bird's ancestry, and on care and maintenance of them by the man in charge. Nature does nothing unnecessary, so does not keep in a state of athletic fitness the hearts and lungs of pigeons which are living the life of garden fantails. This extreme comparison serves its purpose, but there are many intermediate stages. It is improbable that unfit birds are ever sent to a race point, but half-fit birds are — and if the latter ever see their homes again it is after a journey too leisurely to gain honour, glory, or a touch of the pools money. It is on the long road back that the hard questions are asked. About an hour out on the journey the pace-setters are into their rhythm; there may be a head-wind; even if not there will be abundant temptations for a bird to give up the effort if its body signals that it cannot take the strain. Muscles which have not been hardened, lungs which have not been cleared, reserves of energy which have not been built-in by skilled feeding and careful exercising, come between a tiring racer and its dream of home. Below are fields and roof tops, rest, food, water. Small wonder if for him, home tomorrow seems as good as home today, or if tomorrow eventually lengthens into next week, sometime, never.

It is the physical failures which lose races, the non-physical attributes which win them. The capability to find home by the shortest route, the zest and guts to do so as fast as possible ignoring the temptation to 'drop' during the race, are known to flying men as 'brain' and 'heart'. They cannot be put into a racing pigeon by any human agency. They can only be inherited from forbears who themselves rose above the hardships of the road, passing on their initiative and resilience to future generations. A good man can make the best of these qualities in his birds, but he cannot increase them.

In pigeon parlance, brain can be defined as the homing faculty plus the capacity to learn from experience, heart as the determination to maintain all kinds of effort, mental and physical, until reunion with 'home' is achieved. In pigeons with heart, everything is subsidiary to home: tiredness, bewilderment, hunger and thirst are all to be overcome or ignored. In very simple terms, the pigeon with heart keeps going when the rest have stopped or slowed down, and the factor which keeps his heart high is his consciousness of home.

The pull of home can vary between the all-compelling and the mildly desirable. Here is the significance of home being more than just a place. The pigeon's desire to return to it is not founded on blind uncritical instinct. The factors which compose home, in descending order, are first procreation, expressed in the presence there of a mate, secondly security based on the human influence pervading it, only thirdly on the food, water and safety it provides. The first two of these each outweigh the third, which can signify only through the others. No matter how palatial the loft, it is the attraction of the family spirit inside it which provides the impetus for the few extra yards per minute which win races.

Given that the attraction-power of one mate is much the same as that of another (and if not, human ingenuity cannot alter it), the only ways in which the magnetism of home can be increased so that they improve the actual homing effort, is through the ability of the man in charge to create that aura of confidence and sense of all's-well-with-the-world to which a pigeon will be anxious to return — not in due course, but as soon as possible. The best pigeon flyers are men of quiet reliability to which their birds tune in so that when results are assessed over a period, theirs prove the birds which come back quickest.

This pulling power in a flying man is a combination of inborn flair and dedication. Flair of any kind is unknown to its possessor until he tries, and it is probable that more pigeon men than not are agreeably surprised to find that they have it. Pigeon racing is not a sport that can be lightly undertaken; too much preparation, foresight and planning are needed for most people to go it alone. Newcomers to the sport have generally built up their enthusiasm in advance, and learned the basics, by helping out in the loft of a friend. They are likely, therefore, to have seen flair in action.

But even to those who have flair in high degree, pigeon racing remains a demanding sport, perhaps more demanding in terms of commitment than any other sport involving living creatures. This is why it is so well suited to those who are occupationally home-based, and to family participation. A racing loft presents so many aspects in its operation that in many cases some must perforce be shared. There is often need, for instance, for somebody to do the paperwork, somebody else to act as transport driver for the training programme, but there is only one place for whoever cares for the birds — in the loft. The link between man and pigeon grows out of companionship; companionship means togetherness, so flying men spend many hours in or near their lofts, their presence well known to their birds. To be among them while doing the many recurrent jobs that loft management demands, talking quietly to them, accepting their confidence, forges the link.

So much for the physical and the discernible mental characteristics of racing pigeons, and of pigeon men. What of the great mystery, the capability which has defeated all attempts to explain or locate it, the means by which pigeons find their way home. Many theories have been advanced to explain 'the homing instinct'; none, on testing, have been proved correct. But since it is at the heart of pigeon racing, let us look briefly at what is and what is not known about the phenomenon.

First, it undoubtedly happens. Secondly, it probably is not an instinct but a subconscious capability; the difference being between a blind irresistible compulsion to return and an ability to find the way. An instinct, implanted by evolution, would not be confined to a single domesticated sub-species and it is a fact that pigeons in the wild show no great proclivity to return home if taken away from their birth-environment, or even to migrate. The ability to find the way has been ascribed, unsuccessfully, to a number of different influences including electrical influence (using magnetic north as a navigational baseline), the stars (astranavigation, though pigeons fly in daylight only), the sun (direction-finding by solar angulation), and an internal gyro facility (adapting the balance canals of the inner ear). One of them may be right; the best evidence points to the involvement of the earth's magnetic field. But all that matters to flying men is that the capability in fact exists.

And it obviously does. The writer believes that all racing pigeons possess it as a sub-conscious attribute to much the same degree and that the variations in their success at using this capability is governed by the differences of their levels of conscious intelligence (in applying their subconscious impulses) and their determination in pressing the effort to a successful conclusion. In short, brain gives them the route home; heart makes them take it all the way.

The quality of heart corresponds to the same element in human affairs which we know by various names — guts, bottle, grit, bottom, valour, morale and mettle being among them. This is the quality which makes the racing pigeon what it is. It is concentrated more highly into every generation because the breeding of racing pigeons constitutes accelerated evolution. Human judgement mates the best of them to the best and the successes of this process are separated from the failures by the relentless arbiters of racing pigeon destiny, the road and the clock.

3   Life in the loft

Since the loft is more than merely the place where pigeons live, the needs which it must fulfill deserve some imaginative thought before its purchase or construction and equipment are begun. It is the point of origin of its birds, and their invariable destiny. No matter where they start, all their journeys will end there; their training flights, their daily exercise, their races from far away. In the loft they will build up their health, pursue their love-life, rear their young. Their performance in races will depend on the power of attraction by which the loft pulls them home. It must be a paradise for pigeons.

A loft can be large and expensive, with the latest trend in every gadget, yet still not be a paradise. Or it can be small and economy-built but, by reason of the contentment of its birds, be for them a heaven on earth. Let us try to visualize the physical appearance of a loft which provides the essentials, bearing in mind first that it can be enlarged if ambitions or opportunities grow, secondly that however grand it may be it can only be the setting for the race-winning spirit; the spirit itself has to be created.

The word loft, in non-pigeon parlance, means that part of a house between the roof and the inhabited rooms. It is common in mainland Europe, but rare in Britain, for these spaces to be developed to house pigeons. British lofts are normally outbuildings on ground level. Here the word applies equally well because 'loft' derives from the German 'luft' which means air. Even in the shelter of their home, racing pigeons are birds of the air. They require a great deal of it, always changing so that it is never stale. Their priorities differ from ours. Our first need is warmth, theirs is cleanliness, the atmosphere included, and a loft is a building enclosing a great deal of very fresh air.

Because of their thermo-adjustable plumage, in which puffing out the feathers can convert them into the equivalent of quilted clothing, birds seldom suffer directly from cold. But they do suffer from its side-effects such as draughts, damp and frost. The building which best meets the pigeons' basic needs of ventilation without draughts is narrow, divisible into compartments, the upper half of one of its long sides being open to the outer air. Whether it is built of wood or brick is immaterial. It is essential that the semi-open side should not face south-west (whence the wettest and most frequent winds blow) and that the other three walls and roof should be air tight; and desirable that the site should be clear of high trees, telephone and power lines.

Let us enter a loft already in use, to see how this inner world of a team of racing pigeons is designed, what it contains, and why. It is a summer day, at the height of the old bird racing season. Despite the loft's restful atmosphere, all the activities for which it exists are in full swing.

This loft faces east, catching the morning sun. We enter by a door at the side, which gives onto a passageway running the full length of the loft inside the open front. The internal ground dimensions are 18 ft × 7 ft 10 in, (5·5 m × 2·4 m) sub-divided into three compartments on our left, each measuring 6 ft × 6 ft (1·8 m × 1·8 m), the passage being 1 ft 10 in (550 mm) wide. The open half front is made of white-painted vertical wooden dowelling, with weather-boarding below it. Dowelling is one of the basic raw materials of pigeon racing. To instal it is time-consuming, but the effect

A racing loft. Note the forward-projecting roof to give shelter from rain, and the dowelled front for ventilation. At ground level are the externally-serviced feeding troughs for the three compartments.

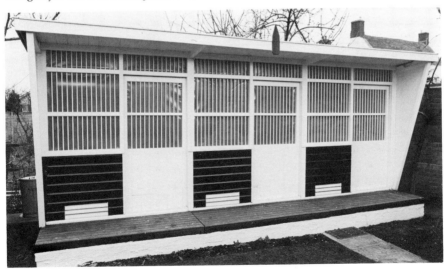

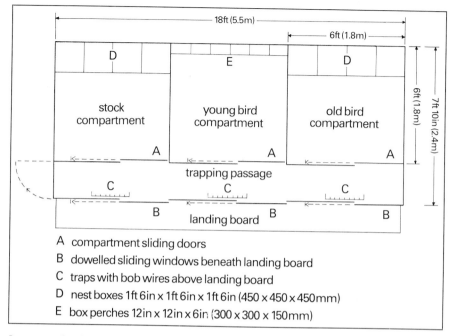

Lay-out of a loft, plan view. Note the internal sliding doors, the nest boxes in position in the first and third compartments, the partitioned-ledge perches in the second.

tidy and efficient. The only alternatives to it are metallic, either mesh or netting. If pigeons fly against or cling to either, serious damage can be done to all-important flight feathers. They cannot cling to vertical dowelling. Because of its eastward aspect the dowelled front can be shuttered in hard weather. Ventilation is then provided by rows of holes near floor and roof level, providing intake of air which circulates without intervening draughts.

Though the door by which we entered is hinged, to give a tight seal, there are no hinges inside the loft. All inner doors are sliders, economizing space and minimizing disturbance. The size of the three compartments is now regarded as standard, and the significance of 6 ft × 6 ft (1·8 m × 1·8 m) with a ceiling at 6 ft 6 in (2 m) is not mere magic. This is the size in which a man of average build can touch all four walls without moving his feet. This enables him to reach and pick up any pigeon anywhere in it without fuss or causing alarm to other birds which at that moment may be perching on his hat, sitting on his shoulders, or preening on his boots. If he is anything of a pigeon man, and they are any good as pigeons, some of them will be doing these things. For reasons to be detailed, the act of picking up a pigeon is of critical importance in the sport.

The datum size of 6 ft (1·8 m) square per compartment decides the number of birds which a loft can hold. The greatest menace in all stockmanship is overcrowding. In nature, predation, infertility or disease reduce the populations of those wild species which grow too numerous for their habitats. In domestication the inevitable sequel is trouble if not disaster, and certainly non-success in pigeon racing. Every form of livestock has its proven density formula. For pigeons this is 3 sq ft (2·80 sq in) of floor space per bird.

A 6 ft × 6 ft (1·8 m × 1·8 m) compartment giving 36 sq ft (33·45 sq m) of floor therefore accommodates twelve pigeons. In practice this fixes the loft's winter strength at twenty-four birds, its summer strength at thirty-six or, temporarily forty or so. The apparent discrepancy arises because racing and breeding are interdependent, so that each racing season adds young birds to the loft's strength. The racing season also entails losses, and some young birds may be culled as being below standard. So the year's pluses and minuses roughly cancel each other out, though most pigeon flyers play it safe by aiming to have a small surplus at the season's end. This enables them to keep only those which show real promise either for future racing or as breeding stock. The seasonally higher number can be accommodated because in summer all three of the loft's compartments are in use, in winter only two.

On this summer day the three compartments are occupied as follows. In the first, second-string racers and some proven stock birds kept for breeding are in the nest boxes, rearing the last youngsters of the year. These 'late breds' are an insurance against the loft being left under strength if bad weather or some other accident causes losses in the current season's young bird races.

Young birds and animals often have great charm. Young pigeons do not, and are far from sharing the attractiveness of kittens, puppies, chicks and lambs. When first hatched they are known as 'squabs', a word which well implies their grotesque, even repulsive nakedness and lack of proportion. When feathered and known as 'squeakers', no explanation being needed, their awkward oafishness seems little improvement. It is miraculous that such caliban-like creatures can achieve the trim athletic beauty of trained birds. Yet the miracle happens, and fast. At fourteen weeks a pigeon can be raced over the middle distances to which birds of the year are sent.

This surprising rate of development is not matched by a correspondingly rapid decline, as generally happens in nature. Racing pigeons, though

How to hold a racer. Maximum contact-area with the hand gives the pigeon a sense of security. Note its calm confidence, and the owner's right hand; the thumb firmly but gently secures the wings, the legs are comfortably couched between first and third fingers. There is nothing for the bird to do except relax and enjoy it.

seldom raced after seven years old, may live on into their twenties. Most breeding compartments contain some ten to twelve-year-olds still renowned for the quality of their offspring, or for special ability at rearing the young of better racers than themselves. Baby pigeons are reared on 'pigeon milk' injected into their crops through the bills of their parents. This milk is precisely what the word says, being produced and stored inside the parental crop and resembling thick cream. As the young bird grows this is reinforced by regurgitated food, the proportion of which increases progressively through the squeaker stage until it entirely replaces the milk. Thereafter the degree of predigestion is reduced until the young bird has been naturally weaned on to normal food.

The next compartment contains a dozen or so earlier birds of the year, all March-hatched and now able to fly. Except for occasional inexpertise in folding their wings, and signs of immaturity in the wattle, they are already indistinguishable to the unpractised eye from adult birds. However, they are very easily distinguishable by a practised hand. The hand is one of the great communication links between man and pigen, which is a reason for the importance of the act of picking-up. There is a way of holding a pigeon, gently but securely cupped in the hand, always with the head turned towards the holder, which the bird quite obviously enjoys as a kind of restful submission, and in which the bond of companionship grows between the two.

In this position the hand of an experienced flyer conveys more information about the bird, its character and fitness, than ever his eye can tell him. The feel of a trained racer, as it sits trustingly on one's palm, is unmistakeable. One senses whether it is relaxed or tense, hence whether calm or excitable by nature. It is cool to the touch, firm against the hold of the thumb across the back. The well-tuned, strongly developed muscles give the impression of a body formed of solid india rubber. This leads to a revealing surprise. Subconsciously, one expects something so solid to be proportionately heavy, but a trained racing pigeon is not. When it 'handles light' despite its strength, a pigeon is said to be 'corky', a sign that the training programme has been effective and well-timed.

Birds of the year are in this respect mere boys among men. They have been kept together in a single age group to make training easier. Being a self-contained squad, these younger birds will not find themselves stretched beyond their capabilities to keep up with seasoned performers, nor will they tempt the latter to fly slower at daily exercise. As the young bird races proceed, their owner will watch their form carefully and, guided by hand and eye, form his opinions as to which are the precocious developers, and which are the potential improvers long-term. But for the present he is still preoccupied with the big events of the old bird programme, for which his best racers of the season are in the third compartment.

They too are in nest boxes but are not rearing young, merely incubating eggs. They are pot eggs, substituted for the real eggs before the parent pigeons began to sit. The impulse to return to the nest and to the procreative functions of hatching and rearing is one of the most powerful elements in the loft's power to impel the homing birds to greater efforts to return, hence the inseparability of breeding from racing.

But the process of breeding is energy-consuming, especially the rearing stage. This also interferes with rest and relaxation because of the need for attentiveness to the young, and the production of pigeon milk diverts the food intake away from the parents' own use. Therefore the normal practice is that birds which are to be raced hatch and rear one 'round' of offspring in early spring before racing begins, and thereafter are prevented from breeding.

However, nothing can prevent the laying of eggs by the hen, nor the fertilization of them by the cock. Nor would the loft retain its power of attraction if a pair which had laid eggs felt themselves prevented from

Nest boxes in occupation. These are designed for the 'widowhood' system for racers in training, in which the hen is penned separately, the cock being given limited access to her. The 'natural' system, in which cock and hen share a nest box with their young, is always used for stock birds, foster parents and, by many pigeon flyers, for race birds too.

incubating them. These processes are allowed to continue uninterrupted so far as the birds are concerned, except that the eggs they sit on never hatch. The eggs they lay generally do hatch, but the hatching is not accomplished by the birds which laid them. Since such eggs have been produced by birds which are good enough to carry their owners' hopes in races and, being in training, are in high physical condition at the time of fertilization and laying, the germs of life which they contain are too valuable to be wasted. When the substitution of pot eggs takes place the real eggs are generally put under non-racing foster parents who hatch and rear the young.

Pigeons lay two eggs for each round of offspring. The idea of a 'pigeon pair', one offspring of each sex in every 'round', is a pleasant myth. The parent cock and hen share the tasks of hatching the eggs and rearing the young. So the early pre-racing 'round' of young does not interfere with the training of the parents, provided only one of them at a time is out of the loft for exercise or for a training flight. Thereafter the laying of eggs by the hen follows a known time sequence in the absence of young to be reared, each further 'round' being followed by its due incubation period on pot eggs.

The outline of a year's proceedings in the loft which, in imagination, we have visited thus becomes something like this. In January the twenty-four pigeons are having their mid-winter rest. Their newly grown flight feathers and cladding plumage for the racing season ahead are now complete, and their constitutions are recovering from the strain of producing them. This is so great that 25 per cent of all the protein that a pigeon eats in its lifetime goes to the making of feathers. Though the total period during which new feathers are replacing old spans six months of every year, late summer sees the process at its peak. It is then that the body feathers are changed in a swift escalation of the moult which maximizes the demands on the bird's resources, leaving a short recovery time before the hardships of winter have to be withstood.

No matter how good their management, housing and food, winter means as much to domestic birds and animals as it does to those in the wild. The greatest adverse factors are the short duration of daylight and the relative absence of sunshine. Under these influences all living creatures, ourselves included, take a short stride towards hibernation, the response of all animate life to lowered temperatures far back in evolution. Physical processes decelerate until the days lengthen and the higher-angled sun enriches the atmosphere again. We all know, indeed feel, the difference of having the sun on our backs.

In the dark January days life is at its lowest. But for racing pigeons the period of recovery from past efforts has ended, and preparation for the future begun. The aim now is to keep the post-moult build-up intact for the coming year's first major development. Breeding is only weeks away. Pigeon racers make protection their priority at this season, protection of their birds from the weather and from all distractions which might reduce the reserves available to meet the energy expenditures to come.

Soon after the last races were flown in the preceding September the newly-bred birds moved out of their own loft compartment and joined their seniors. Little flying takes place in autumn and winter; none until the change of feathers is complete and then only an hour or so of free circling round the loft once or twice a week if fair weather occurs that often. Rain and mist do no good to feathers or to breathing systems, and avian athletes should take it easy in such conditions.

When the age groups joined up the sexes were separated. Cocks and hens to be retained went into separate compartments, the nest boxes being either closed or removed to give more space. The third compartment held the 'spares' until these had been disposed of in various ways, and was then left empty. For several months the two-compartment loft had a monastic air; the voices of the pigeons altered; so did their habits.

Birds which had each been one of a pair became individuals again. No longer sharing nest boxes, perches became status symbols or personal property, each to his or her own. The intimate tones of the coo in communication mate to mate, were replaced by the lower pitched soliloquies of celibates. Not suspended, but reduced animation was the keynote until, imperceptibly at first, the days began to lengthen.

Though winter life in the loft is at lower tempo, pigeon racers themselves have much to do. With fewer demands on their time from the birds, they have a chance to take longer views of the future and to make decisions which will affect their sport for years to come. The chief of these concern the matings for the season ahead. In this there are two objectives. Which cocks and which hens together will produce offspring with the greatest likelihood of success? Which cocks and which hens will fly to each other best? Much consideration, and much consultation of notes and records are needed to establish the wisest combinations of these two requirements. More will be said about them later.

In March, nest boxes are opened or replaced in the loft's racing and breeding compartments, and the actual pairing is done. In the wild, of course, pigeons have their own procedure. They pair for life, or until something happens to separate them, such as disease or death from a stooping falcon. In domestication, man decides.

According to his decisions, each chosen pair of cock and hen are put together in closed nest boxes. Racing pigeons seem naturally inclined towards wedded bliss; indeed the bliss rather than the partner seems the dominant interest; seldom does a hen show disapproval of the mate chosen for her. But sometimes this happens, and when it does a new pairing is generally made immediately because quarrelling, even in only one nest box out of many, disturbs the harmony which is essential to all-round contentment in a loft. For this reason pairings are generally made a few at a time so that any sounds of discord can be quickly detected and located.

Sounds of approval are much more general and also more audible. The loft is filled by the rolling coo of pigeons content in the company of the other sex, soon to change to an even more emphatic pigeon language. Courtship, deliberate and with an objective in view, is first demonstratated by the cock. His voice deepens to a rich warble in an ascending and descending scale. Blowing out his chest and neck he dances, bows and circles round the hen. She responds in the manner familiar throughout nature, of feigning reluctance while being careful not to move too far away. Copulation follows.

This ritual is of special interest for a reason other than its part as the inception of a breeding cycle. It reveals beyond any doubt which birds are in fact cocks, and which are hens. In pigeons no plumage or other differences reveal this. Generally the eye of an experienced pigeon flyer will be right on this point, but not always. There is indeed an actual anatomical difference by which the distinction can be established, but to detect it is a task for a veterinary specialist, and may not be to the advantage of the pigeon.

For practical people the outward signs of a more delicate moulded head and neck, a characteristic look in the eye, a more modest deportment, and generally less robust conformation combine to give an impression of femininity. They are best confirmed by watching the behaviour of birds in doubt. To say that a cock behaves in a male manner, and a hen as a female, may seem maddening over-simplification, but it is as near the truth as words can get. A cock is indeed generally a little pompous and pushing, a hen comparatively demure, and with practice one becomes an accurate judge of the matter without being able to define why.

When the first rounds of eggs hatch, home exercise is stepped up for the parent birds. Their attention being fixed on their offspring, they are unlikely to go too wide on their round-the-loft flights, and are more easily called in when it is judged that they have done enough. A little later, training flights begin. They are known in the sport as 'tosses' and are discussed in the next chapter.

If the last twenty miles of a pigeon race are important, the last yard or two are especially so. It is one thing to get the pigeon home, perhaps perching on the loft or on a nearby roof; it may be quite another thing to get it inside the loft so that the rubber race ring may be taken from its leg and put into the clock. Much thought is given to achieving a swift, uninterrupted entry into the loft, for which the technical term is 'trapping'.

Some lofts have a cage-like trap fixed to the front via which the pigeons enter the loft through light metal 'bob wires', hung so that they swing inwards when pushed, but cannot swing outwards, so that the pigeons which have entered cannot leave. Other lofts have 'drop holes' under the roof. These are so designed that pigeons can enter at a downward angle natural to them, but cannot leave because the same angle in the opposite direction is one that they are incapable of ascending. Whether entrance is by trap or bob-hole, exit will be through a window which is opened to let

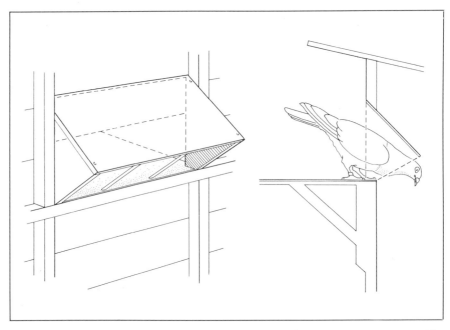

Drop-holes, the way in for mature birds entering after a race or exercise. The side-section illustrates the angle by which a pigeon can enter but cannot leave.

the birds out and closed to keep them in. Of course the window can be left open at all times, if the owner so wishes.

This, known as 'open loft', is now thought to be the most successful method of getting a bird into hand in the shortest possible time. The interval between the pigeon's arrival home and the moment when it comes under human control is governed by the number of decisions it has to make. Decision making (as distinct from reflex reactions to caution, fear, hunger, sex) does not come easily to creatures, bird or mammal. They take their time about it, even when there is no doubt what the decision will be. Watch sheep at a familiar gate, or hens going up to roost. No matter how many times they have respectively entered or flown up, the matter still needs the same length of deliberation. At a trap, pigeons must first decide to alight on the landing board, then to push the bob wire inwards: two decisions. At a drop hole they must decide to stop and enter; one decision. With an open loft they can fly in full-pitch direct to the nest box, for which no decision is necessary.

However 'open loft' brings into sharp focus the greatest danger which confronts owners of racing lofts. This is the threat of invasion of the loft by

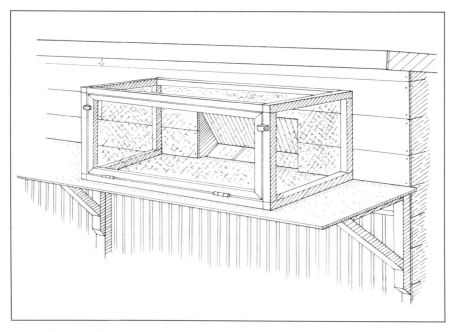

A viewing trap, from which young pigeons have their first view of the outer world, memorizing the surroundings before their first free flights. At the back are bob-wires, through which they learn the skill of dropping into the loft.

cats, rats, foxes, stoats, and ferrets, and even human vandals. All menaces have to be foreseen. A loft can be designed so that it is proof against all animal invasion, but every other precaution should still be taken. To detail them all is not possible. The situation of the loft determines the probable nature and direction of vermin infiltration, and preventive measures vary accordingly.

Human vandalism is rare, but it does occur. The motives are either nobbling, envy, mindless vindictiveness, or sadism; unpleasant though they are to contemplate, these tendencies exist. Lofts which have a successful season, or have a well-pooled bird highly placed in a major race, or contain a big winner, are all vulnerable.

A loft sited in a private garden, or overlooked by other houses, is relatively safe. If it stands remote (as, for example, the many lofts in northern England which stand on allotments) then its safety must be carefully arranged. Perhaps the best and simplest idea is for such a loft to be built high off the ground and surrounded by a metal mesh enclosure inside which an Alsatian dog runs free, kennelled in the space under the loft.

Above left *Calling-in. An owner, tit-bit in hand, brings a bird back to the loft from a home exercise flight. The man-pigeon link in action.*

Above *Partitioned ledge perches, for use outside the breeding season and by young birds. Each one is home to a particular pigeon, re-creating the primeval cave community inside a racing loft.*

Left *Guard dog on duty. A warning voice is invaluable for security, and a Corgi can be relied upon to raise one. For isolated lofts Alsations are a more popular choice.*

Such is the loft, seen merely as a building, like a house without furniture. Inside it pigeons need some home comforts. For the sake of cleanliness these should be essentials only, as few and simple as possible. For half the year each bird needs its own perch or partitioned ledge (the latter is illustrated). Ledges are probably nearer to a pigeon's natural life style, perches are more easily kept clean. Both keep the birds close to the walls when at rest, leaving the centre of the compartment clear and minimizing collisions. For the other half of the year nest boxes are in use. It is better that these should be removed, not merely closed, when breeding ends so as to

A bath set in a lawn outside a loft, and a highly popular institution amongst racing pigeons.

give more space inside the loft during the months when the birds are taking little exercise outside.

Pigeons, wild or domesticated, are idle about nests, so earthenware pans are provided in which the eggs are laid and the young reared. Food and water for adult birds that are temporarily confined to nest boxes, during pairing for example, are given in galleypots, which are earthenware, non-upsetable and easily washed. Otherwise food, grit and water are best provided in troughs and drinkers. Ideally, these should be sited at ground level and outside the wall of the compartment, so that the birds reach it between vertical wire bars on the principle of a cattle creep. This guards the food against being trodden, and against contamination from above. When they drink pigeons do not sip, like poultry and many other birds, but immerse their bills deeply and take long draughts as horses do. They cannot do this if the water level falls too low. Drinkers should therefore always be kept full. What pigeons eat is dealt with in detail later.

Racing pigeons being the cleanest of birds, a bath is essential. Bathing inside the loft inevitably involves splashing and dampness of the surrounding floor, and the inconvenience of providing and removing the bath. A much better way is to sink a bath in a lawn outside, with a bottom shelving to maximum water depth of 2½ in (65 mm). There it is constantly available, and will be much patronized.

So much for the background. Now for the action.

4 The road

The pigeon racing season begins at the end of April, with races for adult birds over about 150 miles. The distances extend as it progresses, leading up to races of 600 miles or more, involving sea crossings. Shetland to southern England and Spain to northern England are examples. In August, when the moult begins for the adults, the young bird races are flown over distances between 75 and 300 miles. Some flyers are chiefly concerned with old bird events, regarding those for young birds chiefly as training exercises. Not all are interested in marathon distances which take more than one day. For almost all, a good 400- to 500-mile pigeon is their chief ambition.

These preferences reflect individual training methods and breeding policies. Men who bring their best birds to racing fitness early, or who possess pigeons which are fast rather than long lasters, are obviously likely to do better over the shorter distances in the first weeks than those whose more patient programmes are designed to bring success after midsummer. Like human athletes and racehorses, pigeons cannot be kept in top form for weeks on end; their training must be timed so that they reach their best on the day of the event at which they are aimed. How this is done involves the racing pigeon's destiny, the road.

The term covers all homing flights, whether tosses or races. It is the last stage of a training process beginning months earlier. To toss pigeons and time them in is exciting and not difficult; the skill lies in first making the pigeons so healthy in body and mind that strenuous tosses do them good, not harm. It is the same story — familiar to boxers, footballers, runners and racehorses — of the build-up followed by the sharpen-up. If basic health is lacking, the exertion of training work-outs will leave pigeons less fit, not more fit, for the tests ahead. The strenuous part of training can only be of benefit if it converts the birds' internal reserves into muscular and nervous energies. Those reserves must be created in advance.

The winter weeks when, to an uninformed eye, the birds seemed to be living comfortably in the loft and doing nothing, saw the foundations laid. Feeding is dealt with in detail in another chapter; all that need be mentioned here is its relationship to training. It can be put in the form of an equation.

Pigeons need a certain amount of nourishment to maintain bodily health. This nourishment is either protein, which develops muscles, bones, feathers and nervous energy (including initiative and will-power); or carbohydrate, which is the fuel to drive wings, body and mind. If, when birds are at rest, too much carbohydrate is eaten that which is surplus to their needs will form excessive fat. This will result in an overload on heart and lungs, and consequently decrease performance. Surplus protein will be passed out as excreta with no adverse effect other than waste of the owner's money. The feeding plan must therefore be to give slightly more of each than is needed to strike a balance between what is eaten and what is needed to keep the bird healthy, warm, and capable of producing fertile eggs and rearing offspring — but not so much more that it becomes overweight.

The traditional formula for this requirement is 1⅛ oz (32 g) of suitable grain and legumes per bird per day. Those who follow it do not go far wrong, provided the grain is suitable and sound. But there is a difference between 'not far wrong' and competitive perfection. Not all pigeons eat precisely this quantity; some need more, others less. As in all stockmanship the hand, the eye, and the intuition born of experience of the man in charge eventually enable perfection in management to be achieved. The aim is that over-wintered racing pigeons should be in full bloom, and just a bit above themselves, when the time comes to step up flying work.

The timing of this presupposes that the birds have paired successfully, and are sitting eggs, and that the weather has settled into a pattern recognizable as spring. Naturally it comes earlier in some places than others. The district, the altitude, the position of a loft all affect the weather factor, and the time taken to get a racing team into shape.

Whenever a fair day gives a chance, it is customary for cocks and hens to have light flying exercise in separate packs during winter. They are allowed to fly for as long as they please, circling the loft in formation with the short sharp wing beats of racers who are enjoying themselves but in no hurry. The return of the hen pack is generally a matter of some relief for the owner; though cocks are sensible enough in winter, hens can be absent minded and stray when not orientated to a nest at home. This light exercise is enough to tone up the circulation and keep the physique in trim.

When the time comes for them to do more, a flag is waved to keep them flying when they attempt to come in. As they become fitter, a pack flies wider circles, still passing over the loft at intervals until called in by the traditional signal of corn rattled in a tin.

Since the rattle of the corn tin is relied upon to bring them in, the pigeons should be hungry when they go out. But not so hungry that their first thought will be to stop exercise and to forage instead. A light feed should have been given, so light that after half an hour's flight they are 'sharp set', and eager for recall. Care must be taken not to overdo the flagging, especially in the early days when, not yet fit, they tire easily. One flagging too many will cause them to sit, resting on a neighbouring roof, watching for their owner to reappear in a more amenable frame of mind, corn tin in hand. Sitting on roofs is the last thing a pigeon flyer wants his birds to do, because it becomes a habit and makes fast trapping impossible.

Keen, healthy pigeons exercise themselves very thoroughly in flights from the loft. In a well-matched pack they adopt their own formation, flying eagerly for as long as required. For this reason only those birds thought good enough to race should be allowed out together. There is an evident contrast between the controlled purposeful work-out of raceworthy pigeons and the half-hearted flapping and gliding of those which are either past it, or just not good enough.

A pack flies at the pace of its slowest member, the remainder idling or fooling about. All lofts have their second string of stock birds, expert foster-parents and old-age pensioners. The first two categories may be the foundations of the loft's success; the veterans may be such heroes of races long ago as to have earned their corn for life. Together they should form a second pack in which they will not hold back better birds than themselves. Later there will be a third pack, when the young birds of the year are on the wing.

After a week or two, regular work-flying round the loft will have strengthened muscles and cleared the wind, so pre-race tosses can begin. They are among the pigeon racer's greatest pleasures — the part of training which improves form, teaches the birds necessary lessons, and enables the owner to learn their characters and qualities as individuals.

Whole books could be written on the planning and execution of tosses. Every flying man has his ideas about them; there are even flying men who do not believe in tosses at all, considering that if their birds are going to do distance flying they may as well have the chance of earning money while doing it — in other words, they are trained in races only. But for the great majority tosses are integral to the sport, and the fact that ideas vary merely confirms that men, not methods, produce winning pigeons. There are several objectives to be met. The first is to increase the fitness of the pigeons by toning up their muscles and improving their breathing; the second, to

A training 'toss' for a small pack of birds which will join up when airborne and fly home in formation. This is the easiest form of training 'down the road' and, at thirty miles or so, a valuable 'sharpener' before a race.

familiarize them with the route over which they will race, especially the final twenty miles; the third, to increase their confidence and desire for reunion with their home background; the fourth, to familiarize them with travel in baskets; the fifth, to settle any doubts in their owner's mind about which of his birds are approaching peak fitness and which are not. There are almost as many ways of achieving these objectives as there are pigeon flyers, and there is much more to it than meets the eye. What follows is an indication of average practices in training on the road.

A toss can be a release of a dozen or more pigeons in a pack, or as 'doubles', or 'single up'. The advantage of a pack release is that the pack will return as a unit, with losses unlikely; its disadvantage is that most of the birds will behave as they normally do in flights from the loft, relying on the follow-my-leader principle to keep together and, apart from exercise, gain nothing from the experience. The advantages of doubles are that without the mass formation of the pack around them, both birds will have to use their brains and initiative while each gives the other confidence. Single-up means total self-reliance; the disadvantage is that as each bird is apt to spend some time circling round, hoping to join up with the next to be released, five-minute intervals are advisable and an hour is needed to dispatch twelve birds.

Single-up, a more testing form of training flight because each bird must be self-reliant in finding its way home. This is how young pigeons are asked the question which determines whether they are fit to race.

Pack releases are general in the first tosses. Doubles and single-up, being sterner tests, are reserved for later, when particular birds are 'asked a question'. The first tosses are over ten to fifteen miles only, the release point being chosen to familiarize the birds with local landmarks and the immediate route home. Some men extend these short preliminary tosses to four, one for each quadrant of the compass. The reason is to spread the familiarization of home ground to all directions so that birds which overfly the loft at the end of a race, or are carried wide of it by wind or by travelling companions, can correct their course as rapidly as possible. Thereafter, release points are extended progressively further along the line of return from the race points for which the birds are being trained.

Care must be taken not to overwork them. Races of all kinds can be lost on the training ground, and there is no way of slowing down a pigeon to ease the strain while fitness is being perfected. So the maximum training distance is generally half the distance of the race in view. For example for a race of 150 miles most of the competing birds will have been trained over seventy miles. Thereafter, as distances increase, the races replace tosses and training flights beyond seventy miles are rare.

The actual organization of tosses permits many variations. The help of family or friends is invaluable, and to spend an hour or so of a sunny

Marking night. The race birds are brought to club headquarters for registration, ringing, wing-stamping, and transfer to the race baskets. Note two clocks on the right; the clocksetters are out of sight.

evening on some open hill systematically sending racing pigeons home is very pleasant. For practical reasons it is generally an assistant who dispatches the birds and their owner who stays at home to time them in, keeping a watchful eye for any dawdlers in trapping. With an experienced dispatcher to record each bird's time of release, doubles and single-ups can be very informative about their relative form.

When the tossing distance has been lengthened along the road about halfway to the first race point, the time has come to decide which birds to send to the early races. In addition to flying form, it is necessary to consider the wing state of every bird, and the stage it has reached in the breeding cycle.

The moult of the body feathers takes place in a comparatively short period of late summer. But the replacement of the feathers needed for flight is spread over the preceding five months. This is Nature's safety-first arrangement. If the primary and secondary flight feathers and the tail feathers were all moulted and replaced at the same time, the bird would be without propulsion, buoyancy, brakes, balance and steerage, and so unable to fly until the new feathers grew. The feathers providing the power of flight are therefore interchanged in pairs seriatim over a long enough period to ensure that the pigeon lacks only one associated pair of them at any time. The primary flight feathers, which apply the driving force, are the chief concern of a pigeon racer. There are ten of them in each wing. They are 'dropped' and re-grown successively, beginning with the shortest pair, which are shed soon after the first round of young have been reared. It is not advisable to race a bird over long distances after the first four have been dropped.

Since both cock and hen share the incubation of the eggs and the rearing of the young, all breeding processes except egg-laying can continue uninterrupted while one of a pair is away for a race. Birds are generally raced while they are sitting on pot eggs (to maintain the attraction-power of the reproduction process) and there are many theories as to when the greatest pull towards home is exerted. Some people believe this to be the tenth day of sitting; all agree that hens which are about to lay, or have laid recently, should not be raced; but whatever the opinion of an owner he will wish to know the exact position of every bird. Hence the importance of a loft diary which notes the laying dates of every racing pair.

Eventually the choices are made, in time for 'marking night' — when race officials receive the birds, mark them, make up the entry sheets, record the pool money, set and seal the clocks and finally send the birds to the race point. Marking nights take place on the evening preceding an inland race, two or three evenings before a sea-crossing race. A room or a building at each club's headquarters is laid out for the formalities. The atmosphere is friendly but businesslike.

Each owner hands in his clock. It is synchronized with Greenwich mean time and started, the exact moment of starting being recorded, then sealed and handed back. Each owner presents his birds for the race, in their basket, to other officials. As each bird is taken out its ring number is checked and entered on the race sheet. The owner pays his 'race money' (entry fee) — about 50p. He is asked if he wishes to 'pool' the bird, states his investment, which is recorded, and pays that, too.

Meanwhile the pigeon's race number is added to the sheet. The rubber race ring, bearing the same number, is put on its leg. An implement with

How the ringer works. The rubber race ring is stretched into a wide open square into which the pigeon's leg can be comfortably and safely inserted. Experienced racers take it without fuss.

expanding claws, known as a 'ringer', stretches the rubber widely so that the pigeon's foot passes easily through it. The claws are then retracted gently, preventing injury. A rubber stamp prints across the flight feathers of one wing the name, address and telephone number of the club promoting the race. The pigeon is then put into a club basket for the journey to the race point.

When all their pigeons have been processed and so have passed beyond their care, the owners generally do what is not unknown among men who have reached the culmination of their efforts, and for whom the future is in the lap of the gods. They have a drink. For the moment there is nothing more that they can do.

But there are others for whom there is now a great deal to do. Marking nights at club level are the small local beginnings of great cumulative enterprises. Long before it begins, a race is getting under way; the organization is on the move and linking up.

5 Race day

Up and down the country the transporters move out. Only the words 'Racing Pigeons', blazoned above their cabs, distinguish them from other motorway juggernauts. But they are purpose designed and fitted out, symptomatic of the sport's scope. Each can carry tens of thousands of birds. Some are operated by private firms, others by pigeon-racing organizations. The Up North Combine alone (based at Newcastle-on-Tyne) has twenty-one of them, with a full-time driving and maintenance staff.

Previously, pigeons travelled to their race points amid the rattle, roar and rhythm of railways. Their journey is smoother and quieter now, just the engine's hum and the swish of tyres. Up front, the driver and his relief are in charge. Behind, where the birds are, the convoyer is in overall command. He is the official who is in charge of the birds, and travels with them to the race point. He takes some of the most vital decisions in pigeon racing, combining the functions of stipendiary steward and starter. He decides not only when and how the race begins, but whether there is to be a race at all on the day in question.

The dread of every pigeon racer, and of every convoyer, is a 'smash' — a race in which serious losses of birds occur. Invariably the weather is the cause, and almost invariably the convoyer is blamed for misreading it, and for not exercising his option to 'hold over' (postponing the race until conditions improve). To help him, every convoyer is backed by a pre-organized weather information network. All Combines have agreements with the Meteorological Office's observatory at Bracknell, Berkshire, which keep them in touch with the developing weather pattern on race days. All race secretaries are allocated a subordinate weather station giving more detailed information locally.

The critical factors are the weather at the race point when the birds are released, and the weather close home when they are finishing their journey. However favourable the outlook at starting time, a convoyer must also

At the race point, the pigeon transporters line up, and their sides are opened. Preparation for the release begin.

consider the possibility of adverse developments while the race is being flown. He can take advice on the telephone whenever necessary, and wherever he is, in Britain or across the English Channel. No amount of care can totally avoid 'smashes', but these precautions keep them as few as possible, and ever fewer as satellite observation and other new techniques improve the reliability of forecasting.

The chief weather hazards are gales, especially when they bring heavy rain, and fog or mist; any of these can develop at the home end without having been apparent at the race point. More menacing still is the thunder-in-the-air situation which heralds the end of a long-hot, dry spell. The atmosphere is then filled with static electricity which blurs the relationship between the pigeon's inbuilt compass and the earth's magnetic field. Mass upsets in navigation may then occur. British lofts become invaded by mystified continental pigeons, and vice versa. Much time and effort is spent by the various national unions in repatriating the wanderers.

Not all, of course, see their homes again. But not all of those which go missing have perished. What happens (especially when electric storms coincide with young bird races, as they often do) is that disorientated birds simply give up the effort to find home and join up with local birds wherever they happen to be. Those that do not fly into the familiar surroundings of a loft become drop-outs with flocks of semi-feral streeters. Flyers do not invariably welcome news of their missing birds, regarding failure on the road as good riddance to bad rubbish. It is a hard doctrine. It is also nature's own law of the survival of the fittest, and sound long-term sense. Now that modern attitudes and veterinary science permit, even encourage, the continued existence of inadequate livestock of all kinds, the uncompromising discipline of the road remains to eliminate potential failures from pigeon racing.

The conveyers' moments of decision are still hours, perhaps days, away when the transporters load up at the collecting centres. The birds await them in race panniers — the big drop-sided baskets which stack together in tiers along the length of the transporters. The transporters also have drop-sides, important at the moment of release. The panniers travel drop-sides outwards and food troughs and drinkers inwards, so that they can be replenished from central gangways.

The journey to the race point is tranquil. For old birds it is nothing new.

Inside the transporter, the central gangway with thousands of pigeons on either side. Such vehicles take birds the whole length of Britain, and across the Channel and part of Europe to release points in southern France and Spain.

Having been through it all before, they soon settle down. The noise and speed of the surrounding traffic seem far away. The air smells sweet from the wood shavings in which the birds are resting. Only an occasional pigeon voice is heard until the transporter rolls on and off a ferry, or stops in a British town writ large in pigeon-racing annals.

The start of a pigeon race, technically the 'liberation', is timed for early morning in races short enough for birds to be home on the day; for early afternoon if a night *en route* is inevitable. The place chosen is as open as possible, clear of high buildings and overhead wires. Often the area of a railway marshalling yard is still used (the link is not quite severed yet), or a cattle market. There in the early light of a summer day the transporters are parked in line astern. The convoyer leaves for the fateful phone calls on which he will base his decision to send or hold. The crew drop the transporter sides and fix draw cords, each of which will open the sides of a whole tier of panniers simultaneously. The pigeons breathe in the fresh air, take in the strange surroundings, and are well aware what is afoot.

These careful, methodical preparations lead to an explosive shattering of

Outside a transporter, draw strings are fixed to open each layer of baskets simultaneously. The layers themselves are staggered, the lowest opening first to minimize risk of injury at the first dash into the air.

The release. Pigeons erupt from the line of transporters, but not yet at racing pace. First they will gain height, then circle in the sky, getting their bearings towards home. Then the race begins.

the prevailing calm. The liberation, when it comes, has a shock effect on first-time witnesses. That gentle pigeons, even in tens of thousands, can produce so violent, so turbulent, so ear-shattering, a release of energy is wholly unexpected. The pent-up energy which is the driving force of pigeon racing is suddenly released. Clattering wings, multiplied and magnified, ascend to crescendo like bursts of massed machine-gunfire; the air rocks and swirls; dust and debris are sucked upwards; the sky darkens momentarily as layer upon layer of flying bodies interlock across it.

The transporters seem dwarfed by the mass of life and urgency and effort which has emerged from them. The cloud of birds swells and swells again as fresh waves of later starters go spiralling up. Then it changes character from something like an enlarged swarm of super-charged bees into a formation flight. The pigeons circle, as if to swing their compasses before setting course, until suddenly the scene empties. The birds shrink into distance; the light returns; by the time the dust has settled again at ground level not a pigeon remains visible of the thousands that filled the sky.

Despite its impact, a liberation is not an instant act, but a cumulative process, carefully controlled. For safety reasons, the panniers are opened tier by tier from the lowest upwards. If all were opened together the down-draught caused by wing-beats from the upper tiers would drive birds from the lower tiers downwards until they hit the ground; or they would be struck and perhaps knocked out by the wings above them.

At first sight it might seem that the tier by tier arrangement compromises the principle of exact equality for all, so carefully guarded by the procedures for clock checking and loft location. In practice this is not so. The race does not start in actuality from the instant when the pigeons first take wing, but from the moment in the circling process when course is set for home. The flight from the panniers is more closely comparable to racehorses going to post than to the burst from the starting gate.

Pigeons do not 'home' along straight lines, but on curves concave to the prevailing wind. This adds a further unknown quantity to their locating process which is revealed as having two stages — first the main journey to the vicinity of home, then the corrected course which brings them to the loft. Pigeons racers, long experienced in watching birds arrive from a race, know that the final approach is upwind and believe that visual recognition is an important factor. Hence the short familiarization tosses from different directions in training.

Though a pigeon race cannot be seen as a complete self-contained spectacle, the sight of pigeons racing is often there for those who know where to look. What happens between start and finish can be pieced together.

The first airborne circles tell the birds the general direction they have to take, and the flow of the main air stream. For pigeons the air is a complex system of currents, some helpful, others barriers to progress. Pigeons are evidently well able to make a flight plan which takes account of them; repeated racing and tosses no doubt make them even more efficient. Having assessed the problems of getting home they then adapt to circumstances.

On leaving the release area they form up in packs of several hundred birds sharing the same general flight line. Fairly early in the journey these packs sub-divide into groups of 150-200 birds who grade themselves according to cruising speed. This sorting-out process probably covers 40-50 miles of the journey. Then begins the stage of the race which establishes the crucial level of ground velocity. The shared flying capability, and the shared destination objective combine to form a common purpose. The pace quickens and, the pack having become a unit, the birds take each other along in the way conditions dictate.

If the wind is helping them, or if there is no wind at all, packs of racers fly high in the sky — sometimes too high to be seen without binoculars. The eyesight of all kinds of pigeon is exceptional, and it is possible that flight at high altitude gives them the advantage of extended visibility. More likely, perhaps, they fly at the level where they find the greatest stability and least interference. Their method of flying in a head-wind suggests that this is their prime consideration.

Pigeons know that when the airstream is against them they go fastest if they can get under it. So they come down nearly to zero height and follow a contour, under-cutting the wind. The proximity of the ground breaks up the adverse airflow, and the contour saves them the energy loss of losing and regaining height. When a south wind blows on a summer Saturday pack after pack can be watched flying down the length of the Pennine fells, only a yard or so above the heather, lifting over the dry-stone walls like steeple-chase horses. They are north-roaders, racing out of Scotland into the Midlands, southern England and south Wales.

The Cotswolds offer another pigeon racing vantage point. The two roads are in sight simultaneously there. A south wind which keeps north-roaders down creates conditions which make south-roaders stay high as they race from southern England or from France to northern England and Scotland. Their apparent speeds are misleading. The north-roaders' 400-mile race into a head-wind will probably be won at a volocity of about 1200 yards per minute — about 40 mph. But a race with a tail wind will be flown at nearer 60 mph; more than 2,000 yards per minute (68 mph) is sometimes recorded. The angle of sight deceives the eye, so that the difference is reversed. The birds near the ground flash past, their wings rippling the air; those remote in the sky seem to make only steady progress.

This is the decisive stage of a pigeon race. It is also the stage which levels out some seeming inequalities. One is the distance factor. When the lofts to which the birds are returning are spread out over many counties, those with furthest to go may seem at a disadvantage, but this is not necessarily so. The winning element is average velocity over the entire journey. Every pigeon race begins relatively slowly. Throughout the initial circling and over the miles in which the packs are joining up and sub-dividing, their pace is still building up towards the eventual cruising speed. Only when the pattern is fully formed do the pigeons get into overdrive, pressing hard for home. Every race also ends with a slower section, in which the birds leave the packs and make their individual landfalls, each to its loft, followed by the minutes lost or gained in trapping. Birds with a shorter distance to travel have the initial advantage of fewer hazards to face. But they also have fewer miles at maximum speed, in which to build up their average, though just as many flown at less than maximum speed.

As to the hazards, most of these fall into the definition 'It's all in the mind'. For its size, a trained racing pigeon is probably the most powerful, intelligent and determined flying organism in all nature, except for some species of falcon. No hundred miles of air, even in high summer, are devoid of risk, multiplied accordingly when several hundred miles are combined in one journey. But storms, headwinds and simple distance seldom produce anything which a pigeon cannot cope with, given its option to descend and take shelter at any time. This option, of course, does not exist during a sea crossing, but since these generally come early in a race they do not constitute a menace to fit pigeons, given the will to cross them.

Given the will. The words express what pigeon racing is all about. The purpose of sea-crossings is not to introduce an element of danger, but to permit races from distances which would be inaccessible if the sea were not crossed. But the decision by a bird to cross it is not one for faint-hearts, and presumably faint-hearts do not try. Pigeon racing is for stout hearts and, with few exceptions, this quality of staunchness is alone enough to raise a pigeon above casualty level.

Undeniably the sport has its losses. It is important to separate the failure rate in normal racing from the disaster rate in a smash. Failure rate means the 10 per cent or so of birds which do not return home in a season; smashes result from situations of such navigational confusion in a single race that good birds as well as bad have in effect no opportunity to return. Fortunately, smashes are rare, but for obvious reasons they are much talked about.

Simple failure to return does not mean that the missing birds have been overtaken by some evil fate. In a small minority of cases, this does happen. But the great majority of pigeons which do not come back have just not tried hard enough to do so. Hence the diagnosis of 'all in the mind'. Lack of concentration on the homing objective, or digression from it as an escape from the stresses of prolonged flight, are the chief causes why the effort to return is not fully pressed home. This is the first stage in the separation of the winners from the losers.

It is easy to imagine what a bird's eye view of the land below may be if the bird is a racing pigeon. In the first flush of freedom and the pull of home, it will not mean much. If there is sea below it will mean even less; little incentive to take a rest there although occasional birds come down on to ships, but generally there is nothing for it but to reach the other side. After that, things may seem different. Suddenly fields and farmyards, houses and gardens, the towns which are always attractive to pigeons, have a new significance. They offer relief from effort which may be growing irksome, an answer to the sharpening question, How much further? It is then that a less resolute bird may 'drop'.

To drop is not mortal sin. It is obviously inevitable on an overnight race, understandable in other cases. But to drop and not resume as soon as needs are satisfied invokes a serious question. Most pigeon racers regard two known and prolonged drops without mitigating circumstances as one too many, and such a bird no longer worthy of a place in the loft. The question is, could any excuse be offered? Weather — thunder storms, heavy rain, low cloud, adverse wind in the area of the drop — might be held to have been bad enough to have made a break in the pigeon's concentration inevitable and therefore not culpable, especially if the journey was subsequently completed. Young birds are generally forgiven their first 'mistake', perhaps more.

Non-pigeon-racers often wonder what action they should take when a race bird drops and stays. Its appearance is enough to tell them that this is no ordinary bird; its streamlined beauty and confiding friendliness are proof enough of that; its two rings are confirmation to the knowledgeable that not only is it somebody's registered property, but it is competing in a race. The procedure, for which every owner of such a bird will be grateful, is simple.

The most likely cause of a pigeon dropping is thirst. If water is put within its reach the bird should drink and fly on within about half an hour. Food should not be offered, because this may tempt it to stay. If, denied food, it stays nevertheless for more than a night and a day, food should be offered and the bird caught. The address of the race-promoting club (which by rule includes its telephone number) can then be read from the stamp mark on its extended flight feathers and the bird reported.

There are very real risks to which the best racing pigeons are as vulnerable as the worst. The chief of them is collision with overhead wires. Though the running of telephone wires underground, instead of overground on poles, reduced this risk, townscapes remain netted by power lines and other industrial cables at heights to which pigeons descend in a head wind. Race birds with their minds on home, and nearing the end of their journey, are especially collision prone.

Next most serious danger is shooting, which causes unfortunate and often unjustified resentment of country people by town-dwelling flyers. Pigeon-shooting must be done in the countryside; woodpigeons are a major agricultural pest. But most of it poses no threat because it happens in early spring, when racing pigeons are safe in their lofts. It is in any case difficult to mistake a racing pigeon for a woodpigeon, and a regular sportsman would be remorseful if this happened. It is thought that most shooting of racing pigeons takes places on the outskirts of large towns, with airguns often involved (weapons which are small threat to moving targets).

A difficult and emotive issue is the killing of race birds by raptorial birds;

in effect, peregrine falcons, round-winged hawks not being fast enough. Pigeon racers are acutely conscious of 'peregrine corridors' such as the Lakeland fells, the north-south axis of the Welsh mountains, and the east-west line of the North Devon and Cornish coasts. Their sport gives pigeon racers a basic interest in all birds and many of them are well-informed ornithologists. They do not wish to see the diminution of any wild species. But the value of winning pigeons (£10,500 has been paid at auction) quantifies their anxiety.

Dangers apart, most difficulties of a pigeon race come at its end. Earlier, a bird's performance depends on getting into the right pack, and staying there. But from about twenty-five miles out its own judgement, exercised unaided, either saves time or wastes it. A high velocity over the main journey can be wrecked by delay in getting the ring into the clock.

The curving course which has brought a pigeon into the home area must be corrected at the right moment to bring it in sight of its own loft. A pigeon must not stay in the pack too long. Large numbers of race birds flying the same line can carry individuals either wide of their objective, or past their peeling-off point. This is known as "the drag', much cursed by owners whose lofts are situated close to, but not on the flight path of birds which have further to go. Hence the value of short distance familiarization tosses on home ground during training.

As a further precaution against 'overfly', lofts used to be painted in contrasted, eye-catching colours. Vivid designs of stripes and patches were worked out — to the scenic detriment of the neighbourhood, as some people thought. Now it is realized that the pigeon's power of distant sight, much more efficient than our own, needs no such emphatic help. The custom now is to keep lofts tidily painted — for appearance and preservation, as much as to make them conspicuous.

Flying men know well when the first birds should arrive from each race point, having made allowance for the weather. Tension mounts at every loft. On some handy shelf the clock stands ready, its empty thimbles ranged beside it. The clock — as implacable a presence as Fate itself — dominates all thoughts until a bird arrives. During this time tactful wives do not ask questions, and favourite superstitions abound. Some men refuse to look at the loft, except out of the extreme corner of an eye; others place a chair to command the line of approach, and sit staring at the sky; some fall silent, some are talkative; telephones ring with news and questions; juvenile cyclists ride through the streets telling rivals that 'Dad's got one'.

Then it happens, with that bewildering suddenness which pigeons can command. At one moment eternity seems in suspension; in the next a slanting shape flicks downwards out of nowhere and 500 miles of speed and endurance ends with a superbly graceful swoop through the open entrance into the peace and calm enclosed by the four walls within.

This is where loftmanship pays off. The pick-up of a wild, flighty pigeon and the removal of the ring is a hectic business seldom remembered with pleasure by either. But where pigeons are easily handled because of their confidence in their owner's quiet management the job is done swiftly and smoothly; no unnecessary action until the thimble with the ring inside it has clicked into the clock. Only a little roughness is needed to turn a tired but willing racer into a reluctant and slow trapper for ever afterwards.

With a ring in the clock, men breathe easier. There will be more to come, and some private formalities as each bird is timed in. First impressions are important, but soon forgotten and a log book in which details of performance, conditions, and any other remarks are entered at the time, before memory fades, is an irreplaceable guide for the future. The returned heroes are looked over carefully and then, fed and watered, left in peace. Their owner, carrying the clock with its fateful secrets, sets off for his club's headquarters.

6   The winnings

When a race has been flown and the clocks returned to club headquarters, the situation is that the result has been decided but is still unknown. It emerges only when the mathematics have been carried out. It is a paradox that pigeon racing, which many people regard as a very simple pastime, in reality depends on an organizational background of immense expertise and thoroughness, and electronic techniques belonging to tomorrow's world. As a consequence, calculations are achieved so rapidly that club results are known within an hour or so of the last clocks coming in. Results at Combine and Federation level, which collate those of hundreds of clubs, take rather longer.

This speed in arriving at results stems from two sources. Pigeon racing has a long history, to which many men capable in other spheres have contributed. When the same sets of complicated calculations have been carried out millions of times over a century, practice makes perfect. Every possible streamlining of the process long since became perfected, the constants are thoroughly established. What seems to be a daunting task, and is indeed a bigger one that confronts any other sport, becomes an everyday thing. Latterly, at pigeon racing's varied levels between homely pastime and national sport, computerization has greatly accelerated every stage. At its headquarters, the computer power which serves the sport as a whole compares with that of a joint-stock bank; at its base, many local clubs now have their own computers.

The end-product of it all is the average velocity of each bird in yards per minute. For this the factors required are the individual distances between start and finish and the duration of flight. The former are established long in advance, the latter is the secret contained in the clock.

Every would-be pigeon racer must first join his local club. Before he can enter his pigeons in races the exact position of his loft must have been plotted by the governing body. Two members of his club visit the loft, bringing with them a 25-in to 1 mile Ordnance Survey map (or, in cases of special difficulty, the 50-in version). This is lined up on local landmarks and checked by cross bearings. The two members then agree on the precise position of the loft, and a pin is passed through the map at that point. The map, with the pinhole ringed, is then sent to headquarters where the co-ordinates of the loft are defined in six-figure eastings and northings. From this map reference a computer renders its latitude and longitude to within two decimal places of a second. Should the loft be subsequently moved, if only ten yards, the location process has to be repeated. Each loft is in this way given its location factor. Every race point is already coded and, using the Great Circle System of navigation, each loft's distance from any of them is arrived at, and becomes a constant in working out its birds' velocities.

The time factor is less stable, because clocks vary, and variation factors are re-calculated for every clock used in every race. All clocks are checked by the officials who set them on marking night, and re-checked against Greenwich mean time when they are opened after the race. Any difference is known as the 'long run variation', because it covers a greater span of time than that occupied by the flight of the bird in the race. The proportion of the long run variation applicable to the flight time is then worked out and known as the 'short run variation' and is added to or subtracted from the duration of flight to provide the time factor. From that, it is only a short step to working out the velocity itself.

In this way the placings in a club race are arrived at. In due course club results in major races are amalgamated into Federation, Combine and National lists, which decide the destination of the money and special prizes at the higher levels. Club prize money is modest. The winner nets £5-£10; second, third and fourth proportionately less for an entry fee (known as 'race money') of 20-25p. At higher levels the rewards are much greater, largely as a result of the recent spread of sponsorship. In the 'National', from Nantes, France, in which 10,000-12,000 birds compete, the money at stake in a recent year was £50,000.

Not that the overall winner gets this or even a substantial proportion of it. The policy in pigeon racing is to spread the prize money in big events well down the list. The top rewards therefore fall some way short of clearing the jack-pot but are still handsome. Enough remains for the first hundred or so also to pick up worthwhile sums.

In addition to the prize money there are 'the pools'. This is the form of fixed-sum wagering whereby owners back their birds in a manner analogous to *pari-mutuel*, the French system of betting on racehorses. In effect it is a 'sweep', in which the participants compete for each other's stakes. In pigeon racing it avoids the less desirable accompaniments of betting at odds created by a market so that, in theory anyway, it prevents the complication inherent in British racecourse betting whereby great benefits can be diverted to gamblers not directly implicated. As a community, pigeon-racers are competing for their own money. Apart from sponsorship they are neither beholden to, nor at the mercy of non-participating financial pressures.

The pools are organized into various money units. Most clubs operate separate pools at 5p, 10p, 15p, 20p and 50p. An owner enters his pigeon by putting its number on the list and paying the sum named. Each bird can be entered in any or all of these denominations. For major races the pools deal in bigger money. The National quotes 20p, 50p, £1, £2 and £5. There is no obligation on an owner to pool his bird in any race; some never do. But the more birds pooled, the more winnings there are. The general practice is to pay out at a flat rate of 20-1 to all 'pooled' pigeons in their order of finishing until the pool is exhausted, a small percentage being retained by the promoting club to cover expenses.

A winning owner hopeful enough to have 'pooled' his successful pigeon in every available denomination would of course have five useful pick-ups from £100 downwards. It is possible that the familiar expression 'to scoop the pools' thus originated in pigeon racing, the 'scoop' which measures corn feeds being a familiar implement in the sport.

Since the pigeons entered for club events may also be entered — and pooled — at Federation, Combine and sometimes other levels too, it follows that many birds (perhaps most) which are clocked-in on a summer Saturday have in effect taken part in two, three or even more races. The formalities of entry, transportation, convoying, clock checking, velocity calculation, results collation and pools accounting could not be carried out except for a very large, well-organized body of trustworthy, efficient, and mainly volunteer administrators. Week-in and week-out they make the calculations on which the entire sport depends, and in which its quarter of a million devotees have such confidence that the challenging even of a minor detail is rare. At the same time they are responsible for the safe custody and disposal of many tens of thousands of pounds of other people's money. That such wide-ranging operations can continue with almost no public awareness is indicative of the standards pigeon-racers set themselves.

No other sport takes place with less scandal and acrimony. Compared with the repeated and tedious disputes which hit the headlines and thus characterize cricket and football, the pigeon racing community have an enviable record for fair dealing, efficiency and good sense. This does not mean that there is any lack of wholehearted competitive effort, or of vehemence in the opinions held. It has already been demonstrated that much money is often at stake. These things being so, it may be wondered how the human element which has created and so long maintained this state of affairs is recruited and organized.

As in all human organizations, those at the top are precisely as good as those at the bottom permit them to be. The foundations of pigeon racing are in the clubs. The repute of the sport depends on the integrity of the club officials, and particularly on the club secretaries. For most of their history, many pigeon racing clubs had memberships in which few could hold a pen, and fewer still admitted it. From that situation emerged a tradition of paid secretaries who were not themselves flying men. They were not paid much, the normal honorarium being about enough to prevent them being out of pocket and no more. What kept them in the sport was the job satisfaction.

Such helpers from outside are rarer nowadays. The age of electronic calculators and other sophisticated office aids, with which modern life familiarize most of us, means that one no longer needs to be something of a genius to run a pigeon-racing club. Almost everybody nowadays has sufficient grasp of the arithmetic. But, to the sport's great benefit, the tradition of administrative help from non-participants lingers on to form a contact point between flying men and the general public.

That the organization has opportunities to break down is undeniable; that it very rarely does so is self-evident. Club secretaries and treasurers are entrusted not only with the affairs of their members, but with substantial amounts of their money. Yet the number of club officials who fail in this trust has been significantly few across the years.

For much of the year the clubs act not only as race organizers for their members, but in a real sense as their bankers. The custom has grown up, and is generally approved, whereby prize money and pools winnings are not paid out at the time of winning, but are carried forward until the season ends. Then, in the dead of the year, when the pigeons themselves are safely wintering, annual dinners provide the occasion for ceremonial distributions of cheques and trophies. The system has the great advantage that since all dues are paid on marking nights, which is when they are incurred, no member can end the year indebted to his club. But his club may very well be indebted to him, and cheques of three and four figures are welcomed at the turn of the year by those who have earned them.

The higher management of pigeon racing is organized on the basis that participants make policy, professionals carry it out. Guidelines and established practices are laid down for the efficient running of clubs, Federations and Combines. Rules are kept to a minimum. There is, however, a strict procedure for maintaining discipline and settling disputes. But, remarkably, the concept of a monolithic governing body, all-powerful and dictatorial, has been avoided. Even the Royal Pigeon Racing Association itself is constitutionally on a par with lesser bodies, wielding only the influence it has earned, with no built-in paramountcy. This is a sport that has never lost sight of the fundamental truths that its participants are in it for their own pleasure, satisfaction and perhaps pride. Therefore the rights of the individual are constantly respected. Its higher echelons exist to help individuals, rather than to impose a collective will upon them.

Since the nature of pigeon racing involves the crossing of national frontiers, common interests are actual, not a high-sounding phrase, and international organization for the various regions of the world is a necessity. In Britain the four national Unions are interdependent with each other and are among the forty national bodies which comprise Le Federation Columbophile Internationale which has its headquarters in Brussels. Since a fundamental function of national authorities is the issue and registration of rings, their activities can be approached from that standpoint.

The Royal Pigeon Racing Association has its headquarters in a country house near Cheltenham, Gloucestershire, and a full-time staff of thirty-two under a general manager. It issued 1,860,000 rings in 1982. The total has been increasing at a rate of 15-20,000 rings a year. To this the Scottish, Welsh and Irish Unions, plus the independent North of England Union add a further combined total of about 800,000 rings annually. So the influx of new racing pigeons each year for the British Isles is near two and three-quarter million. Not all of these take part in races, or are seriously trained. The rings are put on in the first days of a pigeon's life and its potential cannot at that stage be assessed, so the good, bad and indifferent must all be ringed, and sorted out afterwards.

The five British top line bodies maintain contact through the Confederation of Long Distance Pigeon Racing Unions of Great Britain and Ireland. This differentiates them from the relatively small community of short distance racers whose very specialized sport consists of aerial sprints over a mile and a half or so. It is practised mainly in mining villages in northern England where its chief requirement, lofts situated close together and inter-visible, is most easily met.

The Royal Pigeon Racing Association delegates administration, including discipline, to thirteen Regions. These have local autonomy subject to appeal to the Council of the Association, which can be made only after procedures at club and regional level have been exhausted. The Council's thirty-one members comprise delegates from the Regions. Its President and three vice-Presidents serve for a maximum of three years. The Council meets three times annually, sitting for two days at a time, always in Coventry.

Overseas negotiations are all carried out by the Association, and at times represent a considerable work-load, being in essence a diplomatic function. Pigeon-racers themselves often take foreign race points for granted as protected by tradition and among the unalterable facts of life. In practice this seemingly permanent state of affairs is complicated by permit requirements, agricultural regulations, and the wishes of local mayors — more formidable figures in most European towns than their British counterparts. It is maintained by contacts at government and municipal level.

Useful addresses include the following:

United Kingdom and Ireland

Royal Pigeon Racing Association, The Reddings, near Cheltenham, Gloucestershire.

Scottish Homing Union, Bank of Scotland Buildings, Hopetown Street, Bathgate, West Lothian.

Welsh Homing Union, 26 Pen y Danc, Seven Sisters, Neath, Glamorgan.

Irish Homing Pigeon Union, 37 Bellevue Street, Belfast.

North of England Homing Union, 48 Ennerdale Road, Walkerdene, Newcastle-upon-Tyne.

National Union of Short Distance Flyers 15, Columbia Street, Barnsley, Yorkshire.

National Union of Short Distance Racers 53, Withenbank Avenue, Ossett, Yorkshire.

Belgium

Royal Federation Colombophile Belge, 39, Rue de Livourne, Ixelles, Brussels, Belgium.

France

Federation Nationale des Societies Colombophile de France, 54, Boulevard Carnot, 59042 Lille Cedex, France.

East Germany

Federation Colombophile Nationale, 1071 Berlin, Wicherstrasse 10, DDR.

West Germany

Verband Deutscher Brieftaubenliehaber, eV, 43 Essen, Schonelienstrasse 43, PO Box 1792, West Germany.

Holland

Bureau NPO, Maliestraat 10, Utrecht, Holland.

America

American Union, 11612, Monte Vista Avenue, China, California, USA.

Two specialist newspapers cover the sport in Britain. Both appear weekly:

The Racing Pigeon, 19, Doughty Street, London WC1N 2PT.

British Homing World, 26, High Street, Welshpool, Powys (official journal of the Royal Pigeon Racing Association)

The bodies named above are not the only organizations which issue rings for pigeons. Some straying birds may have been rung by societies devoted to other forms of flying pigeons, which do not race, including tumblers, tipplers and rollers.

7 How to begin

Whoever wishes to race pigeons is wise if he remembers two things. First, the sport is open to all; there are no class distinctions, and no obligations except to play it straight, behave sportingly, and to be ready to help in running it. There are therefore no barriers to those who by enterprise and hard work set up a loft. Secondly, this is a long-term operation. Time is needed, it cannot be hurried. Sound preparation is the basis of success; short cuts lead only to disappointment.

Logistically, it is not until the third year after taking the decision to race pigeons that full participation is possible — and only then if all has gone well. Here is a breakdown of the time factors involved in getting going:

Year 1
  Decision to enter sport taken, say ... January 1.
  Four months to buy build and equip the loft, to ... April.
  Early-bred birds of the year installed ... May.
  Trained and perhaps some of them raced ... September.
  Late-bred birds of the year installed ... August.
  Light training ... September.
  Close season.

Year 2
  First breeding year.
  Birds bought in previous year now yearlings.
  Limited racing of them in old bird races.
  Full programme of racing their progeny possible in young bird races.

Year 3
  Birds bought in first year now two years old.
  Full programme in old bird races up to 500 miles.
  Full programme in young bird races for current season's progeny.

Year 4 and after
The sky's the limit.

Such is the skeleton of the starting process. Now to develop it in more detail. The last thing that a newcomer to pigeon racing needs is, strangely enough, pigeons. The first need is the advice of experienced friends, and the second need is a loft.

It is safe to assume that nobody comes into pigeon racing totally ignorant of what is entailed, and wholly without his own ideas of how he will pursue success. The necessary enthusiasm cannot have been engendered without enough contact to have learned the elements. Enthusiasm being infectious, it must have been caught from somebody. It is very desirable that, in the interval while his ambition is catching fire and leading him towards the positive decision to participate, a flyer-to-be should be listening to, watching and helping a friend who is actively engaged in racing. An example to follow is totally essential, and will not detract from the satisfaction of ultimate success. In the early stages going it alone can only delay, perhaps by years, the time when success is attained. Serving an apprenticeship is therefore strongly recommended.

Luckily, this is not difficult to do for those who go about things in the right way. Pigeon-racers are ever ready to share their interest with those they think worthy of it. Most racing lofts develop their little circle of well-wishers and helpers-out. These, by doing odd jobs, carrying out tosses, standing-in on marking night, running the loft during the owner's holiday and, unofficially, beefing up his pools investment on a fancied bird, learn a lot. Some eventually go into partnership, others start up on their own. By such contacts new pigeon-racers are made, which is why the demand for rings increases by up to 20,000 a year. The sport is growing, and this figure shows how.

Of course such link-ups begin in a small way, non-intrusively. Nobody gets far by simply asking to be let into the secret by somebody to whom he is not yet well known. By definition, all sport is competitive; this sport is very competitive and getting more so. Every flyer develops his own version of the established methods, and his own secrets; he is entitled to be sparing in sharing them, and there will be times when he wishes to be alone with his birds. But no matter how jealous they may be about inner techniques, flyers are not reluctant to spread their pleasure, and to help those who wish to join in.

The first real step in becoming established independently is the possession of a loft. Lofts can either be bought, generally in sections to be erected, or built. The advantages of buying are that time is saved and, because commercially-made lofts must stand comparison in quality and price with those produced by other makers, there is not much wrong with those offered by reputable firms. Except, perhaps, the cost. Without doubt, a self-made loft can be built more cheaply, but it is also certain that nothing is more expensive in the long run than a loft which is less than ideal. In addition to, probably, lower cost, the advantages of a self-made loft are that it can incorporate all its owner's personal preferences, and perhaps adapt better to its surroundings.

The choice between building and buying should be governed by a realistic answer to the question whether the would-be builder is capable of making a proper job (see Chapter 2), and whether he is thinking big enough. The man who puts a real millstone round his neck in pigeon racing is the one who starts off by saying of his loft, 'This will do for the time being; we can make improvements later'. However it is obtained, a first loft should be one which can last for all time (even those wear out). It is true that it can always be added to, perhaps adapted to new ideas. But a season's racing can be lost if a loft has to be replaced, and it is always folly to put any form of high performance livestock into housing which is not good enough for them.

Pigeon racing has plenty of successful veterans who seldom tire of telling of the humble ways in which they began. The legend of the pair of birds in a tea-chest nailed to the wall is as familiar in the clubs as the legend of the millionaires who sold newspapers on street corners is familiar in big business. Both should be taken with a large pinch of salt, and something better done. The inevitable question of how much it will cost forthwith arises. In the present times of fast changing money values any quotation of figures would soon be outdated. A better guide is the estimate that an emergent pigeon-racer is standing himself in for an investment not less than the price of a modest second-hand motor car when all the essentials are considered.

Included in this, for instance, is the proviso that the loft itself will not alone meet all the demands made on it. It will contain the pigeons but not their equipment and, pigeon-racing being a summer sport, the problems of winter are easily overlooked until the first winter sets in. A second building will be required to give weatherproof and vermin-proof storage for food, nest boxes out of season, baskets, litter, medicaments, records, nest pans, galley pots, drinkers and the other minor necessaries which accumulate round any livestock enterprise, and spend much of the year out of use.

Throughout the period of providing the loft and its accessories, the mind of a flyer-to-be will be concentrated on the pigeons which he hopes to put into it. Here again, first principles have to be decided, taking into consideration the owner's personal preference, his money, what is readily and locally available, and the trend of advice which he receives from those he trusts.

There are two main options. A flyer starting from scratch can acquire adult stock birds, and breed from them the racers with which he will begin his competitive career; or he can acquire young birds and race them before he breeds from them.

The first course involves the disadvantage that to take over adult birds means 'breaking them' (teaching them to fly) to their new loft instead of back to the loft in which they were reared. Though this is possible, and regularly done, birds thus 'broken' having won races for their new owners, it is not easy, especially for a beginner, and experienced flyers know they must accept losses in the process. So the risk of loading the new enterprise with disappointment at the start is undeniable. If stock birds of surpassing quality are available, a case exists for accepting them (and proportionate losses) and, having broken them to the loft, using them for breeding only, confining their flying to round-the-loft exercise. Some flyers keep especially valuable stock birds as 'prisoners', never allowed to fly free. This requires very skilled management if they are to be fit enough to breed offspring worthy of their background, ideally requiring an aviary in which they can stretch their wings.

The second course, taking over young birds and rearing them in the new loft, means that the question of 'breaking' does not arise. Compared with taking over older birds it is trouble-free except for an unavoidable reservation. Young birds, never having flown, would be unknown quantities except for what their breeding indicates. Even so, the balance of advantage is on their side. Losses will be fewer; the new owner can have a free hand in their development; and since pigeon racing is a team matter between man and birds the link with the first birds to be raced can be formed forthwith, undistracted by an older generation in the loft claiming attention.

Nearly every flyer breeds more birds than he initially needs. The first round of eggs laid by his racing team, two per pair, would maintain the loft's numerical strength if all the young were reared, even if all the parents were lost. Of course not all the young will be reared but, racing pigeons being vigorous birds, losses in the rearing stage are few. Nor, of course, will all the parent birds be lost. But some of both generations will be, and in order to ensure that the numbers at the end of the racing season are in parity with those at the beginning, flyers breed enough young birds from the second and subsequent rounds to enable them to replace every loss. Hence they generally have a disposable surplus from which a beginner may hope to stock his loft.

Established flyers are naturally unlikely to put what they believe to be the cream of their young birds on offer, anyway in large numbers. But until the road delivers its verdict during the training process, the cleverest flyer does not know which actually are the cream, and which are not; he only knows which ought to be, because of their ancestry. But as the next chapter will show, the communal quality of all a loft's pigeons is a more reliable factor than the individual quality of its star performers. Two pairs of early bred young birds from each of three lofts known to produce winners year after year would make a total of twelve birds of similar age which could be reared on and subsequently trained together, with prospects of success if well managed.

But from these, too, there would be losses, since they are inevitable, and must be written off as part of the everlasting selective process of the road and of training flights. However well-bred, not every pigeon reaches its designed standard, either physically or mentally. Time finds them out and there is a big difference between losing a trusted performer which has proved its worth, and losing a youngster which has yet to face the tests which, as it were, separate the men from the boys among pigeons. Whatever the hopes pinned on them, the drop-outs from a racing team are best dismissed as just that, and the gaps in the ranks filled by others. Which others?

Late-bred youngsters are more easily obtained than early-breds. They are too backward to be raced as young birds, and probably too numerous for all to be retained by their breeders. They are therefore readily on offer. But there are reasons for caution. Late-breds pose problems.

Because they are summer-hatched, nearer than normal to the zenith of the year hence also nearer to its decline, the rhythm of their lives differs from that of pigeons hatched with part of spring and all of summer before them. In particular, late-breds at first moult their flight feathers at times which do not suit racing or training programmes. Until these after-effects of their delayed birth dates are counteracted by the passage of time two years later, allowances have to be made for them. Though they are useful for replacing losses, they should never form a majority of a loft's population.

During its development stage a loft which started with twelve early-bred young birds, losing four of them and topping-up with late-breds, might go into its first winter fourteen strong; the remaining eight earlybreds and six late-breds subsequently introduced. Assuming that the sexes split equally, and no winter losses, this would leave a breeding strength of seven pairs for the following season. Allowing for similar rates of loss and for culling, this would probably increase to ten breeding pairs in its third season, with the notional target figure of twelve breeding pairs attained at the start of its fourth season. In modern times these example figures may be pitched on the low side, but they illustrate feasible proportions and indicate some of the problems of management.

An advantage of starting with fewer pigeons than are intended to be kept eventually, is that it enables a new flyer to get his eye in. Dealing with livestock in numbers needs practice. To have individual insight for each of twelve birds, summing up its particular characteristics and being able to weigh up its form, is not easy to those doing it for the first time. As experience grows and the mind develops its techniques of watchfulness and memory systems, fifty or even eighty cause no problems.

When the first dozen early-breds arrive in the loft they are clumsy, gawky adolescents. Unpractised at preening, their plumage resembles ill-fitting suits; tufts of nestling down remain. Wattles are still pink-tinged, eye-ceres lack the snowy whiteness of mature health. They are unsure of themselves, and of each other, a purposeless-looking bunch; in short, ideal material for a new owner to convert to something better by good management and his personal magneticism.

By quiet reassurance, and the obvious fact that he represents the good things of life, he wins their hearts, being careful to rattle the corn tin, establishing the recall signal for the future. Little by little they relate to each other, become less and less a group of strangers, more and more a unit. The apathy caused by unfamiliar surroundings wears away. Bouts of wing-flapping activate half-formed muscles and awaken the desire to fly — first up to a perch, then from perch to perch, finally to perches with a view of the world outside.

In the caves of their evolution, squeakers grew up in half light. Awareness, first of light, then of a distant view, means that minds as well as bodies are developing. One day, timing it as well as he knows how, their owner puts them out in an airing pen on the loft roof. There, in summer sunshine, they take in the landmarks, getting to know the neighbourhood, laying the foundation of that culminating skill, the location of home. In a week or so they are allowed to fly out. At first tentatively, then with growing duration and confidence, they make playful circles round the loft, organizing themselves gradually into a neat formation flight. Muscles harden, bodies strengthen, gaining the clean-cut symmetry of physical efficiency, the wattle whitens, eyes glow, wind and limb knit together as excercise raises the level of fitness, and still their minds are centred on home.

Until they 'fly off'. This is a decisive day in the life of young pigeons; memorable, too, for all pigeon flyers, and traumatic for those who are still beginners. Flying off means a sudden decision to leave familiar surroundings, to go into the unknown and explore it. Instead of the usual tidy exercise circles, the whole pack vanish as if by unanimous intent, and may be gone for hours. The first time it happens is an unnerving experience. Even though the owner knows what to expect, his faith in pigeon-wisdom has not yet been confirmed. To say that their return, as sudden and unheralded as their departure, is a relief understates the case.

What has happened is that youth has had its fling. It is unavoidable, and in the long term beneficial. From this experience the birds develop their stamina and gain self-reliance, going out as babies and returning with a new maturity. When they have done this three times, and before it becomes habit, the time has come for serious business and training begins.

Pigeon racing is full of contradictory time factors, none more so than in the capabilities of a developing racer. It emerges from the egg as helpless as a human baby and much more ugly, unable to stand, lift its head, or feed itself. Yet in less than four months it can race 100 miles against others of its age, having withstood considerable mileage on the road during its build-up in the few preceding weeks.

Within the limits of commonsense, first year pigeons seem immune to overwork. They can fly short tosses of two, five, ten and fifteen miles three or four times a week before the first race. After it, short mileages seem no longer to awaken their concentration, and result in more losses than longer distances do. Conditioning and education of a first-year racer, if short, sharp and concentrated, produces improvements which cannot be attained later. They include toleration of travelling and other pre-race stresses, and the race-awareness which produces the winning streak. Late-bred birds of the year, though too young to race, must have the same training on fine autumn days after the season has ended if they are to develop these competitive qualities.

A year later, the same pigeons need more restrained treatment. Despite their rapid early development, full maturity comes slowly. Yearling racing pigeons, including those which seemed precocious and won races at four months old, are still physically soft in the following summer compared with their seniors, and not yet settled down mentally. The races they have flown have been with their own age group. Few of them are capable of staying 300 miles in a fast pack of seasoned performers; an attempt to do so may leave a yearling overstrained for life, or to be lost through dropping out disheartened. Yearlings which were early-bred are generally raced over distances up to 250 miles only, or else rested for the whole season. Those which were late-bred are little different from young birds. A frequent procedure is to fly them in middle distance training tosses with older birds, and otherwise to confine their yearling season to breeding.

Two-year-old pigeons that were early-bred are treated as fully mature racers up to 400 miles, but are not sent to longer races for a further year. As two-year-olds, of course, their form is fairly well established. Not so that of birds of the same year which were late-bred; they have scarcely raced at all, but sometimes prove top-class when eventually 'asked the question'.

Thereafter a racing pigeon's life can be a long one. Those with speed, durability, stout-heartedness and consistency — always there or thereabouts, and making no mistakes — may fly for six or seven seasons on the road, and be capable of more. But 'may' is written advisedly; pigeons of that quality are too valuable for breeding to be risked over too many years.

Such are the stages through which a newcomer to racing must take his birds before the full sequences of participation are in his reach. When once he has bought his clock, or in other ways has access to one, the road is open to him if he has decided to go it alone. But this is not the only way to start. Partnership with an established flyer is another, and forms a time-honoured strand in the pattern of pigeon-racing, as a later chapter makes clear.

8 Breeding and feeding

Because breeding is integral to racing, the subject can never be absent from a flyer's thoughts. For this there are two main reasons. First, breeding is the normal means of replenishing his racing team, the quality of its annual recruits being directly dependent on the success of matings he decides, and his rearing methods; secondly breeding is a tactical factor affecting the training of his birds and their readiness to race. Whether he is considering the present or the future, he cannot take his mind off breeding. In the same way, both breeding and racing depend on the physical condition of the birds which in turn is partly dependent on what they eat — though not more so than on housing, cleanliness, contentment and exercise. So feeding is also an on-going preoccupation. It is convenient to consider these two never-ending processes in the same chapter, breeding coming first because it involves a greater number of debatable propositions.

Having said that breeding is an unending process, it may reasonably be contended that this is not actually so. For half the year the nest boxes are either closed or removed from the loft. For several months it is customary to separate the sexes. During this time the birds obviously stop breeding. But this does not mean that their owner stops thinking about breeding. He watches and notes the effects of breeding that has already been done, plans the breeding for the future. Basically his aim is that of the breeder of any other high performance livestock, which is to produce peak achievement, whether in the racehorse, the sheepdog or gundog or greyhound, the milking cow or whatever else. But the means by which that aim is pursued vary from one species to another, and there is no breeding problem quite like that of the pigeon.

Among racehorses, mares produce one offspring at a time; the result of each mating in any one year can therefore be assessed precisely. A bitch produces multiple offspring, each one of a litter of six or a dozen puppies producing that number of different combinations of the characteristics of sire or dam; so the results of a mating between dogs cannot be precisely assessed, only argued about. But in the case of a horse or a dog a fashionable sire may cover forty mares or forty bitches, so that his genetic influence is spread through a great number of individuals in all future generations, thereby increasing the risk of breeding 'too close' (with excessive common ancestry in sire and dam). Thanks to artificial insemination, a successful dairy bull can spread his genetic influence even more, and much more widely. But a big winner among racing pigeons is mated to only one hen per year, produces only two offspring per round, and is capable of only three or four rounds per breeding season. His direct influence, compared with that of the sire in other species, is limited both by the small number of hens with which he can be united over a lifetime, and by the small number of descendants which they can produce together.

Pigeon-racers have in only very small degree the option open to such other stockbreeders as can afford it, of introducing the classical blood of the moment to upgrade their birds. No matter how brilliant a racer a flyer may possess, the rate at which his influence can permeate his own loft is slower in terms of generations than the rate at which the influence of a Derby winner can permeate the world population of bloodstock. Pigeon-racing being a team game, it is the quality of the mass not the quality of a loft's stars which produces winners. Hence the importance of foundation stock coming from families of pigeons which, year after year for decades at a stretch, have produced their share (or preferably more than their share) of winners.

Correspondingly, a pigeon-racer has a different slant on the breeding process from that of breeders of other livestock. They, with access to every bloodline anywhere if they can afford it, attempt by careful combination of those bloodlines to produce outstanding individuals. He, able to introduce outside blood only rarely, attempts by skilful use of the bloodlines which he already possesses to produce a community of pigeons of winning calibre in the expectation that some of their number will in fact win. It is less important to him that certain pre-ordained blue-blooded specials shall triumph, than that the overall quality of the whole team shall not deteriorate, and if possible improve with time. So no pigeon unworthy of the rest should ever be retained, lest its weaknesses dilute the strengths of those superior to it when breeding.

As each season's racing goes by, this requirement is largely affected by the inexorable selective process of the road. Put simply, the sub-standards come back late or not at all; the honest and competent are proclaimed as such by the clock. The success of a breeding programme relates directly to the soundness of its raw material, which is the parent generation. These are reasons why no would-be pigeon-racers should begin with rubbish, import rubbish, or tolerate rubbish. It is easier for the level to slip than to climb, and this it will certainly do if slackers are holding back the able workers, either in the nest box or by slowing down the pace on training flights.

The greatest force for good which a flyer can exert on the next generation of his pigeons is by the elimination of those which the clock has proved unworthy to eat corn at his expense. Equally true, the most he can hope for (barring miracles) is that none of his pigeons produce offspring worse than themselves, and that a few produce something better. A man whom the out-turn events proved to have done this for twenty successive years would not be out of pocket, to put it mildly. And, of course, miracles sometimes happen; but as they cannot be banked upon, they are best forgotten until they do.

In pursuing the ideal of a consistently improving team of racing pigeons, a choice may be made between several breeding policies. It will be enough to indicate here some general patterns which each individual adapts to suit himself. Before doing so it is as well to foresee the eventual result of a breeding policy.

If pursued consistently for, say, ten years it will establish in the population of the loft some of the characteristics of a race apart. A form of concentrated natural selection will have been at work in which the pigeons which have produced the best results have also produced the next generation. They will have been those which their owner preferred, and hence gave the chance to make the best of themselves. They will also be those which, with their immediate ancestors, were best suited by the loft, its communal spirit, the feeding plan, its situation, the climate, the emphasis on young or old bird racing, medium or long distances, the training methods and all the other factors which interlink to form the life style of a racing team. They will have acquired a family resemblance (known in the sport as 'levelness'), a character, perhaps a predominant feather pattern which the observant (and all pigeon flyers are observant) will come to associate with their owner. And as the years pass the birds which he has bred will have eyes for him above all others. They will be an extension of himself.

In a real sense the building up of an effective racing team is a work of creation carried out by nature assisted and presided over by man. For those men and women who do such a thing there is an understandable temptation to play at being God. This leads to the most widely followed of breeding methods whereby the owner decides which cock pairs with which hen. The choice is based on careful consideration of the performance, ancestry and characteristics of each, and the owner's growing experience will help him to temper his reliance on what ought to happen, on the evidence of pedigree and performance, with his instinct for what will happen, based on his knowledge of his birds and their forbears. This application of the 'fancier's eye', an intuitive stockmanship, is the personal creative element in the breeding process which gives a man a sense of active participation in the progeneration of the birds he races. It is deeply elemental in the relationship of the man to those birds, and is something which most flyers would not be without. It also has logic on its side in the sense that human judgement in mating the best to the best, or some close variation of that principle, and in avoiding too close consanguinity, should be an improvement on the slow process of unaided natural selection in fostering improvement.

But there are some flyers who achieve excellent results by taking the opposite course. They hold the opinion that human intervention in the selection of mates may do more harm than good. There is something to be said for this. The operation of mutual attraction is not wholly a matter of chance, and coupled with nature's way whereby the most vigorous and dominant male drives off all rivals and acquires the most desirable female for his mate, may well produce the optimum in offspring. So under this principle, the sexes are put together en masse in a loft compartment with an adequate number of nest boxes, and left to decide their own pairings.

But obviously this system (or lack of it) cannot be operated without safeguards. The owner will be as vigilant over the pairings which the birds decide as if he had made the decisions himself, and quick to intervene if he sees an obviously unwise union developing — for instance, a cock driving to nest a hen of closely similar parentage. Whatever method of deciding matings is employed, the pedigree book, in which earlier matings and resulting offspring are recorded by ring numbers, is much in use as a check.

No man in his right mind would use this process of pairing-up (and most of its exponents are very much in their right minds) unless he was in no doubt of the thoroughness of his preliminary culling process. The whole idea is based on the assumption that every bird among the many who are allowed to choose their mates is good enough to mate with any other. In breeding racing pigeons the exclusion of the passengers is more important than choosing the role of those with merit. The latter will make their mark in some form anyway; the former must not be allowed to make their mark at all.

The chief disadvantage of free-for-all pairing is that it makes more difficult the application of the most vital of all breeding considerations, the progeny test. If success in breeding of any form of livestock were even roughly proportionate to mating the best of one sex to the best of another its problems and its fascinations would both disappear, and it would cease to be a matter of skill and care. The reason why the 'best to the best' idea proves to be useless as a formula, though with limited value as a guide, is that the ability to transmit characteristics is as variable as the ability to perform in races. In addition adverse characteristics are as readily transmitted as those that are beneficial.

From a pigeon-racer's viewpoint, successful parents are those which produce offspring of high racing ability, regardless of what they themselves have done. Unsuccessful parents are those which produce offspring lacking ability, no matter how illustrious their own performances were. These undoubted truths are not, however, the end of the story (in livestock breeding there is never an end to the story). For inherited abilities, including the separate abilities of pigeons to race and to produce good racers, are not always passed down from parent to offspring but are likely to miss a generation before recurring in grandchildren.

To try to achieve every facet of the eventual objectives, and to avoid every possible pitfall is likely to require a breeding plan so complex as to be inoperable in the practical circumstances of a racing loft. The distilled experience here summarized produces the outline which follows, every flyer thereafter being free to introduce his own adjustments in his capacity as creator of his team.

First the breeding value of every bird must be established not on the evidence of what it and its ancestors have done in races, but on the evidence of what its offspring do — both as young birds and in old bird races, too. So a firm assessment of breeding capability cannot be made until a pigeon is four years old, when its first crop of offspring can be sent 'all the way' in 500-mile events and longer. Then the distinction clarifies between those parent birds which merely have racing abilities in themselves, and those which can pass on racing abilities.

Secondly a distinction must be drawn between a bird's own ability to produce racing qualities and its ability to do so in partnership with a particular mate — so far as this can be known. The cautionary note is introduced because though the fidelity of mated pigeons is very high, it is not total. Probably a proportion of eggs laid every year in every loft under active racing conditions are the results of extra-marital unions. It is a wise pigeon which knows its own father, and a wise pigeon-racer who makes allowances for this when something uncharacteristic appears to result from a particular pairing.

Thirdly, every calculation must take account of the fact that racing pigeons produce not only children but grandchildren. Breeding is emphatically not a process that can be planned only one generation ahead. Its fundamental principle, that the best breeders descended from the best racers shall produce the birds of the future, is best implemented by flyers who are thinking ahead, not back.

From time to time other guides appear to the selection of the most promising racers and breeding stock. None of them disturb the fundamental priorities described above, but some of them may well help it. Recently, what is known as 'eye-sign' has occupied the attention of many progressive breeders. While there is neither explanation nor scientific proof of its effectiveness, experiences have been reported which include instances of co-relation between eye-sign and long-distance racing performance, and it has been found to be an inherited factor.

Eye-sign, not confined to pigeons, is visible as a fine, shadowy line forming an arc between the forward edge of the iris and pupil (i.e., in the pigeon, the side of the pupil nearest to the beak). It is visible only in light strong enough to cause a reduction in the size of the pupil; a pupil dilating because of poor light tends to obscure the 'sign'. Many investigations made in Europe and America have led to the conclusion that eye-sign is associated with enhanced acuteness of sight, and is hence relevant to route-finding by birds racing at high altitude.

Whatever else may now be thought, and subsequently proved, about eye-sign and similar phenomena, the overriding probability is that this is one of many manifestations of advanced physical development, and that its useful employment depends in turn on advanced mental development. The need for a healthy mind in a healthy body is never more true than it is of racing pigeons. This introduces the importance of nutrition, the raw material of life.

Food includes the substances of which racing pigeons (and ourselves and all other creatures) are made, and the fuel which energizes all activities. In the case of pigeons it gives power to their wings and stamina to their minds and nerves. Strong pigeons fly fast for as long as their impulsion to do so lasts. Impulsion lasts as long as their sense of well-being; and when that fades, only inherent determination can mobilize their remaining resources. So it is necessary that a bird sent to a race shall be at peak physical power, and in a state of confidence and contentment, so as to prolong its willingness and capability for fast flight and to postpone the moment when its last reserves are called upon.

The food intake of racing pigeons therefore divides into building materials (proteins and minerals), and fuels (carbohydrates). Pigeons being vegetarians, these requirements must be met by plant products — beans and grain providing them in their most concentrated form. The basic matter of obtaining them presents a flyer with no problem. All he has to do is pay. Reputable firms serving the sport offer balanced mixtures to meet all

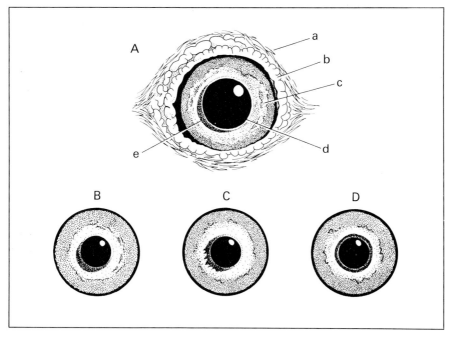

Eye-sign in outline: **A** *the eye as a whole: (a) surrounding feather; (b) the cere; (c) the iris; (d) the pupil; (e) the dark crescent of eye-sign well placed outside the pupil's leading arc.* **B** *crescent placed low;* **C** *indeterminate sign;* **D** *no eye-sign*

seasonal needs. However, such a basic matter as food does not remain simple very long in a sport as competitive as pigeon racing.

The individual, often secret traits of stockmanship which distinguish one man's methods from another's, naturally extend to the vital matter of the rations. Though most flyers feed the proprietary balanced mixtures, most of them use their own favourite additives and variants to suit particular needs and circumstances. Additionally, as would be confirmed by spokesmen for the firms concerned, no set of customers could be more critical of the foodstuffs they buy than pigeon racers are.

The first need to be considered is the protein element, because unless a racing pigeon is soundly built no amount of energy-giving food will enable it to fly fast. On the protein element depends the size and strength of the bird's main powerhouse, that greater pectoral muscle which, one-third of the bird's total weight, drives the down-beat of its wings. On the protein element also depends the quality of feather including the flights which, durable and tempered, are the pigeon's contact with the air. The produc-

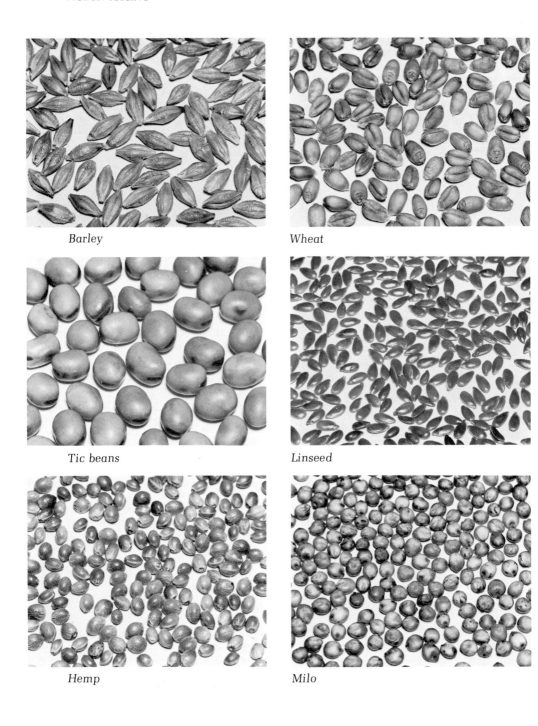

Barley

Wheat

Tic beans

Linseed

Hemp

Milo

Maples

Maize

Left and above Racing pigeons' food (approximately life size).

tion of feather absorbs a quarter of each bird's protein intake throughout the year. Peas and beans are its main source.

The best peas (and the most expensive) are maples, preferably from New Zealand and sun-dried. A seasoned maple pea is so hard that its digestion by a bird seems something of a miracle, but in this case hard tack makes hard pigeons. The peas should be small enough to be swallowed without straining by the birds, round and full and not approaching black in colour. If New Zealand-grown there is seldom likelihood of this, but some English-grown maples are dark enough to be suspect, since their colour deepens in a wet harvest and such a crop may have deteriorated. Tic beans, though an excellent protein source, are sometimes too big for pigeons, but British growers have recently produced smaller varieties which overcome this problem.

The high-mileage months, when training and racing are going on, mean that pigeons need quick energy. The traditional forms of this are maize, small-grained varieties being essential, and oats. Wheat is valuable as the basis of maintenance rations during the months of reduced activity and growth between the end of the moult in autumn and the beginning of breeding in spring. But only as the basis; the bean and pea growth-foods must still be given but in smaller proportion.

The greatest energy-producer, and energy-replacer, of all grains is unpolished rice. It is of great value in the last few feeds before a race, and for the first few feeds afterwards, when a bird is recovering and re-building its reserves. Sometimes a pigeon loses 10 per cent of its weight in a race and special, easily digested foods are needed for quick replacement. Nearly every flyer has his own secret formula for this purpose. Canary seed and such oil-bearing, fat-forming grains as hemp, rape and linseed are much used, as are some pelleted poultry compounds. In America pigeon feeds are made up in pelleted form, and some are available in Britain.

Like all grain-eating birds, pigeons digest their very hard mouthfuls by muscular contraction of the gizzard. So grit must be supplied as a milling agent. It is advisable to buy this in package form, since locally-dug grit may carry infection or contamination by farm chemicals, however wholesome it seems.

9 Great names

Like all specialized subjects, pigeon racing has its verbal shorthand. When flyers meet, their conversation includes technical expressions, some of which have been explained, and recurring names, some of them foreign, the significance of which takes time to understand. They are those of great pigeon men of the past whose skill as breeders combined to make the modern racing pigeon the highly developed species which it has now become — raised genetically, mentally and physically into a different class above all other domestic pigeons.

In the previous chapter, reference was made to the way in which every careful breeder creates in his loft a community of pigeons personal to him, true to his own type, and in every way a minor race apart. Those who did this most successfully in the sport's formative years established their own versions of the racing pigeon. These versions are known as strains or families, sometimes as types or dynasties. They operate in the calculations of flying men as the Bruce Lowe system of bloodstock lineage operates in the breeding of racehorses.

The most influential of them were Belgian, and their influence became dynamic in the decades between 1860 and 1880. Pigeon racing was then Belgium's only national sport, and their accumulated expertise gave them a world lead. The racing pigeons they evolved had no equal as long distance racers in the mild and stable continental climate. In the rougher weather of the British Isles, in the track of oceanic winds and storms, they were initially less successful until adapted by Britain's best breeders. Pigeon-racers therefore sub-divide the thoroughbred racing pigeon population into types designated by the names of their Belgian originators and/or those of the Britons who developed them. Here are the names of the tribes of racing pigeons talked about in everyday speech and often recognizable in appearance, the Belgians first:

Grooters

Several members of the Brussels family of this name achieved fame. Their pigeons combined quality and power. The head of a typical Grooter is distinctive in robustness of skull, in the alert, sensitive, intelligent eye, and short stout beak. The wing is strong, the primaries broad. A grizzle feather pattern combined with Grooter blood is held to indicate high racing character.

Delmotte

This line, subsequently carried on by a flyer named Jurion, was of smaller but very tough birds. Their capacity for work and training is such that they are said to fly best for hard men. Blue, blue chequer and mealy are the characteristic colours.

Hansenne

A bull-necked, strong-headed, cobby type of bird; muscular and stout in constitution. Colours generally dark, with a bronze sheen to the feathers.

Gits

A breeder in Antwerp of great wealth, and strong individuality. He once declined an offer from the English breeder Logan of the 'two finest carriage horses in England' for any two of his birds. Their influence on British pedigrees is now very strong, a century later. Gits breeding is sometimes indicated by feathered legs.

Wegge

Another Antwerp line, notable for very large pigeons, mainly blues and occasionally reds.

Gurnay

A line that persists in pedigrees because its quality of bringing out the best in other blood makes it especially valued as an outcross. Usually dark in plumage with a reddish tinge to black feathers.

Barker (N.)

This Yorkshireman, who became a naturalized Belgian so that he could deal in property there, was a rival of the Grooters and a brilliant breeder. He also bought and sold widely, and exported many birds to Britain.

Those who did most to develop them in Britain included:

Logan (John W.)

Logan bought many birds from Barker, the two doing more than any to establish a British type of racing pigeon, Belgian-based but able to cope with our testing Atlantic weather.

The Royal Lofts

King Edward VII started racing at Sandringham with pigeons given to him by the King of the Belgians. Details are unknown, but they would have been the best available. They were managed successfully by J. W. Jones, a local schoolmaster. The King and his successor George V were generous in sharing their blood with other leading breeders.

Wadsworth-Wilson

A founding father of the sport in Britain, his line still exists in Lancashire. Its birds have a reputation for stamina and determination but not for early development, often delaying flying to their true form until three years old.

Bryant

A pioneer in adapting Grooters blood to British racing conditions. The usual colours of his line are the strong ones of blue, red and dark chequers.

Thorougood

Also very old established. Its basis was a numerically very large stud, affording many variations within the original strain, hence great genetic vigour.

Stanhope

A line of big, strong birds — lengthy and with extra-broad tails. Not notable for producing sharp youngsters, but specifically long-distance pigeons; often said to be not merely flyers but racers.

Baker (J. L.)

A line of smallish pigeons, dark in colouration — blue chequers, black and chequer-pieds.

Toft

Often dark red chequers. On the big side, and much used by breeders to give substance where needed.

Osman

Three generations of this family have maintained a line characterized by dark red chequers and mealies. Colonel Osman pioneered the Army Pigeon Service in World War I. Osman pigeons are notable for balance, strength in the back and shoulder, and absence of exaggeration elsewhere.

Clutterbuck

This line of stalwart, cobby pigeons noted for feather quality was raced successfully by their originator and on his retirement from the sport was sold almost en masse to Sir George Dewar, so being kept as a unit for longer than most strains.

Barker (J. W.)

Dr Barker served throughout World War I in the army, which interrupted his racing activities at a crucial point. His birds were renowned both as racers and for their good looks. He won many show prizes with birds that were genuine performers on the road.

10   The human element

In any activity worth the name of sport, to which pigeon racing is outstandingly entitled, the character and quality of rivals and rivalry are crucially important to the individual participant. When he takes the plunge and decides to join in, he would be a fool if he did not ask himself, Who am I up against? What kind of people? What weight of money? What sort of spirit? The great names of the previous chapter are milestones in the growth of pigeon racing, which has changed outwardly since their days, and goes on changing though its inner spirit does not. To answer the foregoing questions is impossible without briefly sketching the background.

History cannot tell us who first raced pigeons. The earliest pigeon racing, in our context, was on the European mainland in the post-Napoleon decades. Those were pre-railway times, so race distances were short by our standards. But they were commendably long for those days, since the birds were taken to their race points in panniers stacked on A-frames strapped to the backs of relays of porters. These hardy fellows carried their loads of pigeons far enough for the sport to reveal its fascinations, though the possibilities which our generation takes for granted were then undreamed.

Probably those long-ago flyers were offshoots of the columbarian societies which originated such European fancy breeds as Norwich croppers, skanderoons, Antwerps and carriers, and imported oriental breeds from the Levant and India, some of which had existed for at least 1,000 years. The pigeon, ever man's oldest friend, had become a cult throughout the continent, including Britain, even earlier, but only for show. Pigeons being small and light, they were sent to shows by stage coach long before agricultural shows were thought of, and more than 100 years before the first dog shows. But the pioneers who were to spread the Asiatic enthusiasm for pigeon-breeding through the industrialized West were centred on the Low Countries: Holland, Belgium, northern France and western Germany.

Immigrant weavers brought it to Britain; others took it across the Atlantic when racing had superseded showing as the predominant interest. In the meantime, the sport had escalated from the A-frame stage to that of sophistication, helped by the interest of scientists and soldiers. The former included Charles Darwin who originated the theory of evolution by natural selection; the latter were concerned with the age-old military role of pigeons as carriers of messages.

Now every developed country has a strong pigeon racing tradition. The heartland, what is now NATO Europe and Britain, have the cachet of being where it all began. Nobody can say where it ends, because it still spreads. North America has taken it up with true transatlantic thoroughness. In South Africa, with strong Dutch and British traditions, it is as major a sport as anywhere. In all the former British Dominions it thrives. Beyond the Iron Curtain, despite security regulations, pigeon racing is recognized as a communal sport, especially in Poland, Czechoslovakia and Russia. In Japan and even remote and tiny Hawaii there are pigeon racing organizations.

Under all these varied cultures the atmosphere of the sport is notably constant. One might say miraculously so, except that the constancy is no miracle but inevitable. The nature of the sport calls for the same commitments and responses, so attracts the same sort of people, wherever pigeons are flown.

Primarily and obviously, it is a leisure pursuit. Its followers must have leisure from something, and industrialization gave it to them, if not much at first. By its basic character, pigeon-racing must always be home-based; not only for the pigeons. This has imported into it the strong element of stability referred to earlier, especially the family spirit permeating its participants both inwardly and outwardly, binding them together into a coherent community. Many pigeon-racers compete as families, all pigeon-racers feel for other pigeon-racers something akin to blood brotherhood.

The social and economic changes have not affected the community's working class nature. Yet the sport's appeal and participation-range has never been exclusively that, and as the barriers crumble they become less and less so. But this has not altered the egalitarian flavour which now emanates more from sportsmanship than from income group or class origin. History indeed reflects the underlying facts.

Some occupations have always in themselves dictated the choice of a stay-at-home sport. In the old days industrial occupations in general did not provide enough money to enable wage-earners to go away from home; hence pigeon racing's working class majority. Other occupations anchored to their homes the people who performed them; hence the traditionally strong infusion of flying men from certain professions and trades outside the industrial orbit. Most of them were those who had to be on call for the rest of the community and the annals of pigeon racing are studded with doctors, pharmacists, parsons, builders, shopkeepers, publicans, garage proprietors, dairy farmers who had to be on hand for milking, smallholders with stock to feed and nobody to whom to delegate the job.

Under modern pressures the catchment area for pigeon racers is widening. That aspect of present day life known as 'the rat race', its endless travel and obsessive stresses, is causing more and more business men to turn to the sport for relief. It has the virtue, denied to most others, of giving more than mere relaxation, a negative form of deliverance which, if required, the bottle can provide unaided. Pigeon-racing fulfills the real need, a total alternative absorption. The result is the filling of a gap in the composition of the sport's devotees.

When World War II ended this consisted of the solid foundation of blue-collar workers plus the smaller element of occupational stay-at-homes and a very small minority of the very wealthy, such as business tycoons and farming magnates who, having by some lucky encounter become addicts of the racing pigeon, maintained large studs with professional loft men in charge. The scene now has a richer variety, and a new energization.

In a recent year at least five flyers were bringing their birds to club headquarters on marking nights by Rolls Royce. They were self-made men from pigeon-racing families who saw no reason why their acquired wealth should separate them from the pleasures among which they had grown up, and from which they had not become separated in spirit. For such men the racing pigeon is not only the poor man's racehorse, but the rich man's too, and they see no advantage in making a change. Professional loft men are not yet an endangered species but, since the real reward of the sport is not success in it but personal participation in that success, they are employed only by those whose affairs render totally impossible its greatest attraction, day-to-day association with the birds.

One pigeon racer undeniably insulated from the day-to-day association is Queen Elizabeth II. From her loft near Sandringham she races as a member of her local club and, with a single non-operational exception, neither distinctions nor concessions are given or expected. The Royal Pigeon Racing Association arranges that, in addition to their normal serial numbers, her pigeons wear the royal cypher EIIR on their rings.

If ever a sport included all sorts and conditions of men and women, this is it. Like all sports today its horizons are widening as its standards rise and, while its attraction at grass roots remains fresh and undimmed, it gets ever tougher at the top. In tune with the times everywhere else, sponsorship by big-time commerce is helping to raise the level of ambitions. In the hotbeds of the game — the London area, the West Midlands, the North-East, South Wales, and the retirement area of southern England, competition grows more intense, the rewards greater. Races are enriched by thousands of pounds. The National Flying Club, only one of many race-promoting bodies, pays out £50,000 per race in prize money and pools. Another race, the National from Nantes, France, was worth £61,000 in 1982. Valuable prizes in kind, including motor cars, are also offered.

This expansion, simultaneous with some difficulties not previously encountered for many would-be flyers, is re-shaping the future of pigeon racing. The chief difficulty is that with the need for satisfying recreations never more urgent, especially in towns, the physical obstacles to participation are increasing. The trite term 'inner city deprivation' has application here. The real deprivation is from contact with nature, of which pigeons are a manifestation. A flat in a tower block is no place for a loft; some paternalistic councils, visualizing only monotone man in their own image, prohibit any pastime beyond their understanding. Pigeon racing is often one of these. The accident of residence becomes a greater barrier than the initial cost.

The two combine to produce ingenious solutions to the problems they present — solutions which go far to explain the sport's growth in an era which might seem more likely to see it outmoded. The idea of sharing spreads. Traditionally, sharing meant two or more flyers running a loft in partnership. Now there are variations on the theme. It is possibte nor two or more flyers to share a loft and race the birds in it against each other. To strong individualists in more happy circumstances, this may seem likely to put a heavy strain on human nature but it can be, and is being done. For those who are young and eager, but faced with residential or financial difficulties, there may be no other way. It is only an extension of the time-honoured custom of near neighbours sharing a clock.

For some with an ambition to race pigeons these stratagems are not enough. Difficulties can be overcome with time and persistence, disabilities are for ever. Yet they do not deter. The help the sufferers are given by other flyers has a way of making all things possible. Lofts are designed to admit wheelchairs. One renowned flyer is blind; indeed it was when blindness, cutting out his other activities, made him perforce home-based, that he activated an ambition of his youth and set up his loft. He has bred, trained and sent out many winners, none of which he has ever seen. The touch that reads braille can read ring numbers; he knows each bird by its feel as it sits in his hand, and by its voice as it joins in the talk of the loft. The pigeons, gentle and confiding towards man, do the rest for him. He has reached the top-flight of flyers.

At that end of the scale, where big money flows in reach of well-established and successful flyers, the pursuit of ultimate success sharpens the pace of innovation. New practices, tighter specializations gain adherents year by year. One example is the 'widowhood' system of race-bird management. Here the cock leads the monastic life of the more dedicated human athletes, seeing his hen only occasionally, the energies normally devoted to domesticity being concentrated and deflected into race performance. Another is more detailed exploitation of breeding. The blending of ancestries has become as exact a science in pigeon racing as in horse racing, and the money paid for the blood of big-winning families escalates.

This has introduced another new element into the sport, the gene bank. This is an imaginative response to one of the flyer's greatest problems, security. The risk of vandalism through human pettiness, such as wantonness and envy, was always there, as we have seen. The influx of big money has multiplied the risk of theft through human cupidity.

The flyers' position can never be easy. Until it has won or nearly won a big event, a racing pigeon is worth only a few pounds, except to its owner. When it has won, or gone close, it may be in the £10,000 class. Such a bird, living among the others in the loft, is a hot property and its temptation-effect a source of anxiety. The big breeding studs were shrewdly set up to provide a solution when their proprietors saw the money escalating. Their function is to buy in big winners of both sexes, which thereafter never race again. They are kept in high security aviaries, paired to each other, and their progeny are sold to the pedigree-hungry exponents of modern high-level breeding. In this way some successful pigeon racers recoup on the enhanced capital value of their winners in the way that racehorse owners do. At the same time a 'market' is created in leading modern strains.

The influence of high finance has not undermined yet the cosy comradeship which pervades the sport as a whole. This flowers most evidently in the close season. When the weather degenerates into winter, when the road has relaxed its discipline, and the next season is still a distant prospect, the social side brings together not only the flyers but their families too. The celebrations are governed by as many traditions as the sport itself. Club dinners and prize distributions, often unpretentious in their style, are major occasions in the life of pigeon people. The shows, over which many purists of the road shake their heads knowingly but still attend, are at least as much social gatherings as competitive. Latterly the reunion factor, too, has been escalating like all else.

Being home-based is not nowadays a matter of financial constraint for most pigeon-racers. Travel agents in all countries have realized that there is no need for them to be home-based outside the racing season. So pigeon tours are now organized to and from Britain, continental countries and America, in which visits to famous lofts are part of the attraction. The idea has been extended to pigeon cruises in spring, carefully timed to bring the voyagers home in time to pair their birds for the season ahead.